From
Shore to Shore

A personal pilgrimage through Wales

Mike Perrin

BRYNTIRION PRESS

© Mike Perrin
First published 2000

ISBN 1 85049 166 6

Unless otherwise indicated, Scripture quotations are from the
Holy Bible, New International Version (1984) used by
permission of Hodder & Stoughton Ltd.

Cover photograph: Mike Perrin
Cover design: Phil Boorman @ burgum boorman ltd
All photographs and maps: Mike Perrin

Published by Bryntirion Press
Bryntirion, Bridgend CF31 4DX UK
Printed by Creative Print & Design Limited

This book is dedicated
to my grandchildren.
May their lives be enriched
by delight in the land of Wales
and their souls by devotion
to the Lord Jesus Christ.

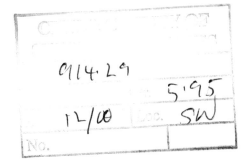

Contents

Foreword

It is not difficult to have a bird's-eye view of Wales. A country as small as this is just big enough to get to know in a lifetime. The hordes of holidaymakers who flood in every summer testify to the shrewdness of these visitors from Europe, America and Japan in recognising a beautiful land when they see one. For those fortunate enough to live here, one lifetime is just enough to travel on every A road and most of the B roads, climb every mountain over 2,000 feet, bounce pebbles on every lake, swim in every bay, catch a glimpse of all the native fauna, and photograph every waterfall.

The point is this: every part of Wales is small enough to know and to care about. Our acquaintance with it increasingly makes us concerned for its life and future; we cannot divorce ourselves from it. Imagine trying to feel the same way for an adopted land. I lived in America for three years, staying most of that time in Philadelphia, a most beautiful city, though with areas which look as if they have been blitzed. I have enjoyed every part of the vast continent of America I have seen, its cities and coastline, its mountain ranges and rivers. But Wales has it all together, at a family scale, with all the additional and observable failures of a family.

Michael Perrin has made Wales his own adopted land, and in this fascinating book he describes a walk from the north coast to the south, which took him three weeks. He opens up our land to you and describes the places he sees and the people he meets with a fine affection. You are as exhilarated as he is

9

when he finally reaches the Bristol Channel, walking onto the beach up to the water's edge, mission accomplished.

This book will give you a deeper love for Wales, its geography and spiritual history. It will also suggest to you some of the reasons why it has become the civilised and gentle country it is today, and how a few years ago there was an additional pervasive spirituality that enriched the whole nation, touching the lives of many of its inhabitants.

Aberystwyth   *Geoff Thomas*
May 2000

Acknowledgements

Grateful thanks are due to all those whose suggestions, advice and encouragement proved invaluable both in planning the journey and in preparing this account; notably John Aaron, Derrick Adams, J. Elwyn Davies, D. Eryl Davies, Gwilym Humphreys and Phil Thomas.

Also to Eifion and Sue Davis, Ted and Joan Holmes and many others whose friendliness and hospitality along the way made this walk so memorable.

Finally to Elaine my wife, who unselfishly remained at home in order to post parcels, monitor progress and dispense advice over the telephone, and whose welcome on my return home made any fatigue or footsoreness more than worthwhile. (Rumours that she is now encouraging me to walk around the world are totally without foundation!)

Mike Perrin

Glossary of Welsh Words

bwlch	gap, pass
cwm	valley
ffugenw	pseudonym, *nom-de-plume*
hiraeth	longing
llygad	(literally) eye; also used for the source of a river
Sais	Englishman
trên bach	small train (on narrow-gauge railway)
tŷ	house

(Other words are explained in the text)

Llanfairfechan
Cwm Eigiau
Pen y Gwryd
Cwm Orthin, Tanygrisiau
Trawsfynydd
Cwm Nantcol
Dolgellau
Abergynolwyn
Machynlleth
Pumlumon
Pont Rhydgaled
Rhayader
Abergwesyn
Rhandirmwyn
Llandovery
Talsarn
Cwm Twrch
Lliw Valley
Loughor
Swansea

Introduction

This is the story of a journey. A journey of almost two hundred miles, along trout-streamed valleys and over windswept and frequently trackless hills; through sleepy, slate-clad villages and busy city suburb. Necessarily a lengthy journey requiring quite a few days to complete, but one for which detailed planning would be difficult with little knowledge of what might lie ahead.

The idea seemed simple enough—to walk the length of Wales, using map and compass, tent and sleeping bag, from Llanfairfechan on the north coast to the Gower Peninsula in the south. Possibly the hardest part—that of finding a suitable and fairly continuous route—had already been done by others.[1] But this undertaking would be far more than just an interesting and energetic holiday, and certainly was never seen as an excuse to add to the growing number of excellent guidebooks available to those planning long-distance walks through Wales.

In part the journey would reflect my very real indebtedness to and love of the land of Wales and its people. When so many folk must be content with the occasional holiday visit, I consider myself blessed indeed to have spent so much of my life, both in childhood and as a working adult, in this beautiful land. Horrendous though the conflict of 1939–45 undoubtedly was, my father's contribution to the war effort required him to supervise Italian prisoners of war held in a camp located at Henllan, midway between Llandysul and Newcastle Emlyn. As a family, therefore, we were privileged to spend those years of world tumult amid the tranquil beauty of rural Ceredigion (Cardiganshire). Fishing for brown trout in the local tributary of the Teifi. Climbing to the top of our 'mountain' (all 629 feet of it!) which, through childhood eyes, seemed to rise like some alpine giant opposite our home in Aber-banc. Sitting by the huge inglenook fireplace in nearby Parc Farm, listening spellbound to old Mr Morgan, whose tales must have rivalled the *Mabinogion*. Even attending the village school, where I learned my first Welsh from the delectable Miss Jones, whom I vowed one day to marry! These were among my early recollections of a land I quickly grew to love. And to it I was so happy to return with my wife and family in 1965 to establish the Christian Mountain Centre in Beddgelert; and then ten years later to become the first pastor of a newly formed evangelical church now meeting in Capel Fron, Penrhyndeudraeth. Today, with Welsh-speaking grandchildren being brought up in the shadow of Mynydd Preseli, little more than twenty miles from Henllan, the wheel appears to have turned almost full circle. And now, whenever we have need to cross Offa's Dyke and travel into England for whatever reason, it is not long before *hiraeth* gently calls for our return.

It is therefore to express something of this affection and gratitude and sense of 'belonging' that I embark on this walk (even if, having been born a *Sais*, such feelings of national identity owe more to adoption than to natural birth). I also want to explore more fully a country about which, in spite of all the years I have lived in it, I still have much to learn. In the time spent working at the Mountain Centre I became very familiar with Welsh landscape, particularly that of the north. However, whether we survey the rugged mountains and broad estuaries of Snowdonia, or the rounded grassy moorlands of pastoral mid-Wales, or wonder at the wave-formed rocks of the Pembrokeshire coast in the west, or even travel the once grime-encrusted valleys of the industrial south, with their now silent pits and rusting steelworks, we are but looking at the anvil upon which the Welsh nation has been forged and fash-ioned. It is the men of history I would know more about, and particularly those men and women mightily used by God whose lanes I would walk and homesteads I would visit. They have long since moved on to a better country (ah yes, there is such a land, better even than Wales!)—'a heavenly one', a place in which 'God is not ashamed to be called their God' and where 'he has prepared a city for them' (Hebrews 11:16). But the fragrance of their memory lingers, and the record of their achievements under God can still challenge and inspire. Surely it is the duty of any that are concerned about the future to spend some time at least examining their past. 'Listen to me, you who pursue righteousness and who seek the Lord: Look to the rock from which you were cut and to the quarry from which you were hewn', wrote Isaiah in another age and context (Isaiah 51:1). But there is truth in such words today and, encouraged by such an exhortation, I set out on this journey.

Perhaps some of the events to be recorded may be interpreted as modern 'parables' from which some lesson or other may be learned. Other observations may relate to the more distant past but still provide us with either a solemn warning or a shining example, which we would do well to take to heart. But enough by way of introduction! It is time to begin . . .

---

1   I am particularly indebted to John Gillham's excellent and most attractive book, *Snowdonia to the Gower*, published by Batton Wicks, formerly Diadem Books, and also the Cicerone guide, *A Welsh Coast to Coast Walk*, by the same author.

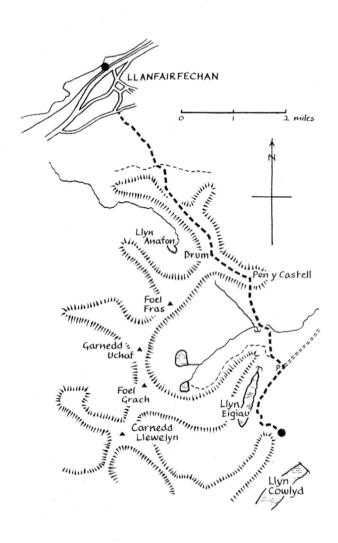

LLANFAIRFECHAN

0   1   2 miles

N

Llyn
Anafon

Drum

Pen y Castell

Foel
Fras

Garnedd
Uchaf

Foel
Grach

Llyn
Eigiau

Carnedd
Llewelyn

Llyn
Cowlyd

1

The journey begins

We stood together on the otherwise deserted platform and watched the train as it disappeared round the bend westward towards Bangor and Holyhead. It had taken us only a couple of hours to reach Llanfairfechan by rail from our home near Porthmadog. The next train I planned to catch would hopefully be leaving Swansea Central in approximately three weeks time at the start of my return journey back to Minffordd. Elaine, my wife, had been much involved in the planning of this coast-to-coast walk, and I was glad to have her company at least for the first few miles. She helped me on with my rucksack. Weighing little more than 30 pounds, hopefully it held all I would need to survive comfortably in the wild for the duration of my journey. I recalled the occasion a year before when, whilst walking part of the Pembrokeshire Coastal Path together, our seven-year-old granddaughter who joined us for one stage had nicknamed us 'the Snails' because, in her words, we 'moved so slowly and carried our home on our backs'!

Although it necessitated walking in a northerly direction to begin with, our first objective had to be the beach. I had already dismissed from my mind the suggestion of one friend, who thought I should carry a bottle of sea water taken from the Irish Sea to empty into Swansea Bay! I really could not see the significance of such an act, and, considering that I had already cut half the handle off my toothbrush and removed the cardboard covers from my Ordnance Survey maps in order to reduce the weight I was carrying to an absolute minimum, it did seem slightly foolish to carry even the smallest bottle.

We walked for a while on the boulder-strewn seashore and took the mandatory photographs. The sun was struggling to shine through a layer of high cloud, whilst a stiff breeze off the sea fully extended the red dragon proudly emblazoned on the green and white of the Welsh flag that was flying from a pole on the promenade. To the north-east, beyond the steep quarried hillside of Penmaen-mawr, the limestone peninsula of the Great Orme was clearly visible, whilst away in the north, Ynys Seiriol appeared to float on the silver-grey sea off the eastern-most tip of Anglesey. Better known as Puffin Island after the colony of seabirds associated with it, this lonely place was home to St Seiriol in the fifth century, a man whose spiritual reputation prompted Saxon invaders to give it the name of Priestholme. Perhaps his reasons for choosing such an isolated place to live were not so far removed from those that prompted me to undertake a walk through countryside at times just as lonely. To know a stillness and solitude in which God's presence may be enjoyed and his voice heard can be of untold value in a world of unceasing activity and stress.

By now the mountains to the south were beckoning, however. It was already approaching lunchtime, and with at least eight miles scheduled for the first day, involving a climb of over 2500 feet to the summit of Drum, it was time to be on the move. We made our way under the busy A55 and up through the town towards Nant-y-felin, but the streets through which we passed held little interest for us; our eyes were firmly focused on the horizon-wide range of hills that lay ahead, rising in places to more than 3000 feet. Indeed, by the time the metalled road was replaced by a rough mountain track (GR682738) we had already gained 300 feet and enjoyed extensive views over the town and far along the north Wales coast.

Reaching Garreg Fawr at 1150 feet, we were ready for lunch. Sadly, this was also to be the point at which Elaine would have to turn back if she was to catch a train home that day. We ate some food and then prayed together, asking God to watch over each of us while we were apart. In a loving relationship no period of separation, however brief, is totally painless, and when one of you may be passing through potentially hazardous terrain alone, it is all too easy to worry. As Christians, however, we believe that 'our times are in God's hands' (Psalm 31:15), and that we can therefore safely entrust one another to his care in the knowledge that he will be with us. Nevertheless, I have to admit to a sizeable lump in my throat as, once we had said goodbye, I watched my wife growing smaller by the minute as she made her way down the hillside and finally disappeared from view. To put things into perspective, it would be all of two days before I would see her again—but then I have always been a sentimentalist!

The path continued to climb steadily in a south-easterly direction, passing beneath two rows of unsightly National Grid power lines supported by pylons, which seemed to march like aliens from another world across an otherwise unblemished landscape. Ironically, the route taken by these also happened to be that chosen by the Romans, whose legions also marched between Ro-wen and the Menai Strait nearly two thousand years earlier.

The col between Foelganol and Drum was soon gained and the scenery changed dramatically. Views of the north coast with its popular resorts and recognisable landmarks were replaced by range upon range of wild and seemingly trackless hills. To the south-west the ground fell away steeply to Afon Anhafon 800 feet in the valley. Before long the small tarn from which its water flowed and which shared its name could be seen, its inky blackness reflecting the sombre slopes of

Llwytmor, Foel Fras and Drum which towered above it. A herd of semi-wild ponies that roam this remote region grazed the mountainside, seemingly unaffected either by the ruggedness of their environment or the steadily increasing strength of the wind. It was three-fifteen when I reached the top of Drum (2526 ft), and the circular stone shelter close to the summit cairn provided welcome respite from the wind, which was now approaching gale-force. Presently two walkers joined me. They had set out that morning from the Ogwen Valley and spoke of gusts which threatened to lift them from the ridge between Carnedd Dafydd and Carnedd Llewelyn.

Such information quickly determined my own route from that point onwards. Having already ascended two and a half thousand feet I was understandably reluctant to descend immediately, especially when one of the finest ridge walks in Wales beckoned from the south-west. But I had to find a sheltered place in which to camp that night and, with rain as well as strong wind forecast, this was not the time or place for heroics (or stupidity). The one hundred square miles of the Carneddau is still considered to be one of the last great wilderness areas of Wales. Over the years far too many have been lost or injured in these mountains and paid dearly for it. I vividly recalled some of the prolonged searches I had been involved in years before as a member of SARDA—the Search and Rescue Dog Association. The length of time it had taken us, for example, to locate the wreckage of a Cessna aircraft that had crashed; or the hours spent struggling through deep snow in 'white-out' conditions searching for a group of lads reported missing whilst on their Duke of Edinburgh's Gold Award expedition. (Following this specific incident, this particular area was officially stated by those responsible for the scheme as being 'unsuitable' for any Duke of Edinburgh Award expeditions.) This is not country to be treated with anything but the greatest respect, and on only the first day of my journey there seemed little point in taking unnecessary risk.

My plan, therefore, was to descend west-south-west from Drum on a vaguely discernible sheep track to Penycastell. Heading south from here will lead one down to Afon Dulyn, where a bridge enables the river to be crossed at a point where water from Llyn Dulyn and Llyn Melynllyn flows via a tunnel through the mountain to Llyn Eigiau. It was my intention to reach Cwm Eigiau myself (though not by means of the tunnel!) and find somewhere to spend the night. A gated water company service road contours around the eastern flank of Clogwyn yr Eryr to meet the metalled road which comes up from the village of Tal-y-bont in the Conwy valley and which terminates at this point. From here, a rutted track leads in a south-westerly direction into Cwm Eigiau.

It was this path I now followed, until I reached the northernmost end of a relatively shallow lake and all that now remains of the fifteen-feet-high dam constructed in the 1920s to contain the water of Llyn Eigiau, a new storage reservoir. By enlarging Llyn Cowlyd to the south and creating a new reservoir in Cwm Eigiau it was hoped to supply the aluminium smelting works at Dolgarrog with much needed hydro-electric power. Unfortunately the dam was constructed on a totally inadequate foundation of loose glacial moraine. Under the immense weight of the dam and the pressure of water behind it the gravel began to shift, and on the evening of 3 November 1925 the dam burst. Tens of thousands of tons of water flooded the wide valley of Afon Porth-llwyd before being funnelled with devastating force down the Dolgarrog gorge. Rocks, some weighing in excess of 200 tons, were picked up by the water and hurled against the cottages below. When the water poured into the smelting works, furnaces exploded, showering the workforce with molten metal. Sixteen lives were lost that fateful night—a figure that would have been much higher had not many of the villagers been in the local cinema located away from the path of the raging torrent. Even so, in a community numbering little more than five hundred people, there were few families in Dolgarrog that night that had not lost a loved one or a home in the tragedy.

I stood by the breached dam and tried to imagine the fearful force that was unleashed when such a huge volume of water burst through the concrete wall. I thought, too, of those down in the valley whose lives ended so abruptly, without warning or time to prepare for eternity, and I recalled the solemn warning contained in the Bible that 'While people are saying, "Peace and safety", destruction will come on them suddenly . . . and they will not escape' (1 Thessalonians 5:3). The devastation which overtook this little village is not to be seen as God's judgement upon those people, as if they were any worse than others whose homes and lives were spared. Rather, it should remind us all that such disasters, either natural or man-made, can and do occur, and that not a single one of us can ever know the precise moment when we might be hurried from this life into eternity and the presence of God.

Situated toward the southern end of Llyn Eigiau stands a remote homestead—Hafod-y-rhiw. A small wind generator whirred away on the roof, whilst the stream which had been diverted to flow alongside the cottage drove a cleverly designed turbine blade. I greatly admired the dogged determination and ingenuity of the person or persons who had chosen to live in such an isolated place and would have very much liked to talk with them. Although the door stood ajar and there were obvious signs of habitation, nobody responded to my knocking or calling. Perhaps they had deliberately come to dwell in such a place in order to escape from unwanted

24

intrusion. Whatever the reason, I left them to their lonely existence and started up the steep hillside behind the house.

By now it was evening and in the overcast conditions light was beginning to fade. I needed to find a sheltered place in which to camp and headed first east and then south-east on sheep-tracks in the general direction of Llyn Cowlyd. The rugged slopes of Pen Llithrig y Wrach rose darkly on my right and were quickly swallowed up by swirling cloud. The very name—Slippery Head of the Witch—seemed designed to send a shiver down the spine. Of greater concern to me, however, was the apparent lack of any suitable ground on which to pitch even the smallest tent. Both above me and below, the hillside tumbled down in a succession of rocky steps interspersed by tangled heather and bilberry.

Then, just as the first drops of rain began to fall, immediately below the remains of a drystone wall, and no more than twenty paces from a small, crystal-clear stream, I almost stumbled upon a patch of level ground. Ten feet by five, with grass close-cropped by sheep, it was perfect. Soon the tent was up, water was collected, and from the warmth of my sleeping bag I was stirring a pan of chilli-con-carne as it simmered away on the stove. The last of the daylight faded as I thanked God with a grateful heart for his protection and provision. The rain had ceased. Only the music-like murmur of the stream and the bleating of a lamb lower down in the cwm as it sought the whereabouts of its mother broke the silence. It was just nine o'clock, but having covered ten miles of rough terrain that afternoon, I was soon drifting into restful sleep.

Distance walked: 10 miles.

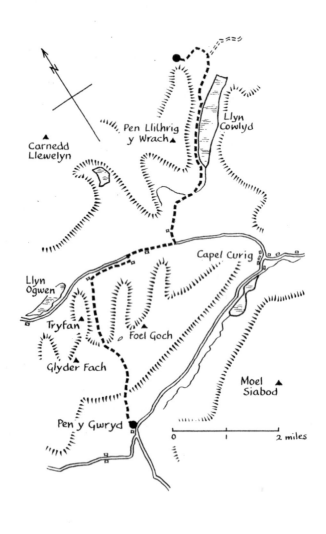

Carnedd
Llewelyn

Pen Llithrig
y Wrach

Llyn
Cowlyd

Llyn
Ogwen

Capel Curig

Tryfan

Foel Goch

Glyder Fach

Moel
Siabod

Pen y Gwryd

0   1   2 miles

2
Glyder Storm

It had rained intermittently during the night, and patches of mist now hung in the valley to add to the greyness of an already overcast dawn. My own 'special' breakfast recipe of porridge oats, raisins, sliced banana and honey, washed down with two mugs of tea, helped to lift my spirit considerably, however, and by eight-thirty I had packed my rucksack and was on my way.

There was no sign of the footpath marked on the map, but numerous sheep-tracks converged on the farmstead of Garreg-wen and within an hour I had reached Llyn Cowlyd and joined one of the two possible routes taken by the Roman road known as 'Sarn Helen'. This road linked Roman forts between Caerhun, near Conwy in the north, and Carmarthen in the south-west of Wales. Today, no one can be sure whether the main route followed the Conwy valley via Trefriw, passing Llyn Geirionydd on its way to the fort of Caer Llugwy situated between Capel Curig and Betws-y-coed, or took the more direct line past Llyn Cowlyd. Certainly the track from above Dolgarrog to Llyn Cowlyd is one of great antiquity, and it is easy indeed to imagine Roman legions marching along this remote but beautiful highway.

Since less disputed sections of this pathway will be joined later on in my journey, a brief explanation of the name 'Sarn Helen' may be of some interest. The late William Condry in his book *The Snowdonia National Park* suggests that whilst *sarn* means a 'causeway' or 'paved road', 'Helen' is most

27

probably a corruption of *y lleng* which means 'the legion'. Plausible enough, but a more appealing explanation is to be found in 'The dream of Macsen Wledig'—one of the stories of the *Mabinogion*.

Macsen Wledig was emperor of Rome when he dreamed of a beautiful lady dwelling in a distant land. So vivid was the dream that envoys were despatched to search for the maiden. Eventually, in a castle near Caernarfon, they found Lady Elen (later corrupted to Helen), whose appearance matched in every detail the woman in the emperor's dream. Travelling to Wales, the emperor married Elen, who persuaded her new husband to build a sorely needed network of fine roads across her native land. This is said to explain the existence of numerous Roman roads across Wales and how the name 'Sarn Helen' has become associated with many of them.

Although my journey did not take me through Llan-rhychwyn (GR775617), it is near enough to warrant mention, since the church there is claimed by some to be the oldest in Wales. The Roman historian Tertullian had reported in the second century that Christianity flourished in places that had never been subdued by the Romans. Furthermore, when the rest of Britain returned to paganism following the departure of the Romans, it was here in the west that Celtic 'saints' continued to preach and set up small churches. The word *llan*, meaning an enclosure, was usually associated with a church. Hence Llanrhychwyn literally meant 'the enclosure of the church of Rhychwyn'. Established in the mid-sixth century, a regular worshipper at the church was Llewelyn the Great, whose court was at Trefriw. Unfortunately his wife Joan, daughter of England's King John, did not appreciate the walk up so steep a hill each Sunday, so Llewelyn built a church for her in Trefriw!

From Llyn Cowlyd my own path descended downhill now for more than two miles, crossing the A5 at Helyg, a stone building sheltered by conifers. Belonging to the Climbers' Club, and located but a short distance from the impressive east face of Tryfan, these premises have a special place in the annals of British rock-climbing history. I intended to traverse the Glyders by Cwm Tryfan and the Miner's track. It is perfectly feasible to reach Llyn Caseg-ffraith (GR670583) by following the ridge, Braich y Ddeugwm, which starts behind Gwern Gof Isaf farm; but with the weather remaining unsettled, opting for a more sheltered ascent seemed to make sense—a decision that was subsequently vindicated. Crossing a bridge over Afon Llugwy allowed me to take the old coach road westward, which seemed preferable to inhaling traffic fumes along the A5, and I soon reached Gwern Gof Uchaf farm and turned south up into the cwm. It was by now lunchtime and, having eaten, I lay on the grass and closed my eyes.

I must have dozed off, for thirty minutes later I awoke to see an ominous-looking bank of cloud spilling over Carnedd Dafydd and Pen-yr-helgi-du from the north. In less than half an hour, at a height of 1800 feet, the first drops of rain were falling. Tryfan on my right and the Glyders ahead were quickly swallowed up in a dark mass of swirling cloud. I had no alternative at this stage but to continue, even though visibility was reduced to 20 yards as the cloud closed in. The wind and rain increased in intensity by the minute. By now any semblance of a path had vanished, and the unstable slope of scree up which I scrambled seemed to grow ever steeper. Then, just as it appeared to merge with a near vertical wall of rock streaming with water, I stepped onto the Miner's path, which comes up from Ogwen via Bwlch Tryfan. Once used by the men of Bethesda, who regularly crossed this range to mine copper above Llyn Llydaw within Snowdon's great 'horseshoe', it was a path I knew well and was especially glad to join on that particular afternoon.

Up on the plateau at a height of 2500 feet the rain was no longer falling vertically—it was driving horizontally before a savagely gusting wind. This area is notorious in bad visibility, with its lack of discernible paths and mud-filled peat dykes, so carefully setting a bearing of 175 degrees on my compass I pressed ahead. Thunder rumbled in the distance and I had no wish to be found on such exposed ground in an electrical storm. It didn't take long to reach the eroded gully that marks the beginning of the descent to the Penygwryd Hotel, and after much slithering and sliding, skidding and stumbling on greasy rock, eyes almost blinded by the rain, I reached the welcome warmth of its legendary hospitality—a roaring log fire and a pot of tea for one, from which I succeeded in extracting five cups!

Like Helyg in the Ogwen Valley, this famous inn has also frequently featured in British climbing history. It was used as a base by members of the 1953 Everest expedition, both for planning and the testing of equipment beforehand, and subsequent reunions following their success. While my waterproofs dried in front of the fire I looked at the signatures written on the ceiling—names which read like a veritable who's who of mountaineering—John Hunt, Edmund Hillary, Tenzing Norgay . . .

Then, my daydreaming over, thoughts turned to the more immediate need of a suitable place to camp in this rain-sodden and windswept part of north Wales! I looked at the clock in the entrance hall. It was getting late—ten minutes past six to be precise. Just below the clock a bus timetable advertised the launch, only two weeks earlier, of a new service between Betws-y-coed and Porthmadog. Only three buses a day, but the next one going down to Porthmadog was due to arrive at Penygwryd at 1840h! In little more than an hour I could be at home soaking in a hot bath and anticipating a night in my own bed, before using the same bus service to return by nine thirty-five the following morning to resume my walk. What more could I ask for?

I recalled with grateful thanks the words of Isaiah 65:24—'Before they call I will answer; while they are still speaking I will hear.'

Distance walked: 10 miles. (Total 20 miles.)

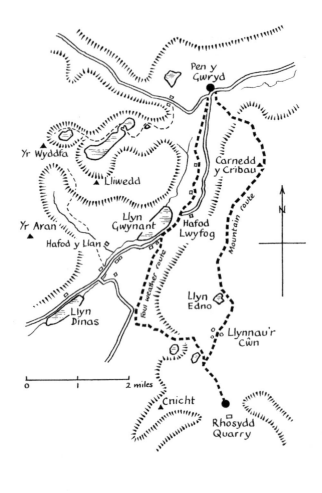

Pen y Gwryd

Yr Wyddfa ▲

Lliwedd ▲

Carnedd y Cribau ▲

Mountain route

Llyn Gwynant

Hafod Lwyfog

Yr Aran ▲

Hafod y Llan

Foul weather route

Llyn Edno

Llynnau'r Cŵn

Llyn Dinas

N

Cnicht ▲

Rhosydd Quarry

0   1   2 miles

3
Nantgwynant

The rain was still falling as I returned by bus to Penygwryd the following morning, but I was glad to be starting the day with dry clothing and equipment. Had the weather been better, it was my intention to ascend the hillside opposite the hotel and follow the ridge over Carnedd y Cribau down to Bwlch y Rhediad and along Cerrig Cochion to Moel Meirch. This is a classic route and one I have always enjoyed walking. There are also splendid places to camp, either by the small tarn on the summit of Carnedd y Cribau with its magnificent view of the Snowdon massif, or by one of the three idyllic Llynnau'r Cŵn or 'Dog lakes' (GR661487). However, this route is also extremely wet underfoot, even after a prolonged spell of dry weather. It was on Bwlch y Rhediad on 10 January 1952 that an Aer Lingus DC3 flying from Northolt to Dublin crashed, killing all twenty-three people on board. So marshy is the area that by the time any rescue teams reached the scene of the crash, most of the aircraft had already been swallowed up by the peat bog, rendering the recovery of all but a few bodies impossible. The ground was subsequently fenced off and designated a place of burial.

With so much rain having fallen during the previous twenty-four hours of my walk, common sense suggested that I follow a less demanding route. In any case, those extensive views for which a boot full of water might seem a small price to pay on a clear day would never be visible with cloud down to less than 1000 feet. I therefore took the old road past Gwastadannas farm down towards Nantgwynant.

This area evokes special memories and will always mean a great deal to my wife and me, along with all those that helped establish the Christian Mountain Centre back in 1966. Hafod Lwyfog (GR653522) is a farmhouse of great antiquity, with records of its existence dating from at least 1558. In 1638 it was the home of Ifan Llwyd (or Evan Lloyd), a strong and well-built man well known as a friend of the poor and oppressed, whose sympathies during the Civil War lay with the Royalist cause. One day, returning from a journey, he found his house occupied, and his food and drink being consumed by a detachment of Cromwell's men. Quietly gathering up their arms, which had been left outside the door, he carried them from the yard and threw them down the hill below the house. He then returned and with his own bare fists swiftly sent the intruders on their way. History is silent as to any consequences of his action. The soldiers, assuming they managed to retrieve their weapons, would more than likely have chosen to keep the story to themselves, both to save their embarrassment and to spare them from likely disciplinary action.

Elaine and I first stayed at Hafod Lwyfog in 1964. The following year in the early summer we returned with a group of young people from the church in East Suffolk of which I was then the minister. We walked, rock-climbed, shared in fellowship and richly enjoyed together the magic of the hills. During that week the concept of a Christian Mountain Centre was conceived. Seven months later we were to leave East Anglia for a new home in Beddgelert, in order to see that vision become a reality under the hand of God. As I made my way down the road I recalled those exciting days and thought of the many young people over the years whose lives were significantly changed as a result of visiting the Centre.

As I approached the lake and looked down the valley, thoughts of an even greater work wrought by God came to mind. As frequent squalls sent white-flecked waves scudding across the surface of the water, between the showers I could just make out the whitewashed buildings of Hafod-y-llan farm beyond the fields at the far end. It was in this homestead that an event took place that was to have widespread repercussions throughout this part of Wales. Unrest in Europe created by the Napoleonic wars had brought a degree of unfamiliar prosperity to the area. The mines and quarries flourished, and the price of agricultural produce rose. People became more materialistic and increasingly sought after worldly pleasures rather than those things relating to God. The churches, weakened by division and controversy, seemed powerless to halt such a trend—that is, until one Sunday evening in August 1817, there in Hafod-y-llan.

A small group of farming folk from Nanmor and upper Nantgwynant had gathered to listen to Richard Williams from Brynengan preach. Few were expected from Beddgelert, since the great John Elias was preaching in Tremadog that same Sunday evening. What followed is best described by D. E. Jenkins of Porthmadog, who wrote at the end of the nineteenth century:

> The service itself began very quietly. Nothing unusual was felt during the devotional part, but as the preacher proceeded with his message, heart after heart became absorbed, while the preacher was being gradually swept from truth to truth. A feeling of intense awe possessed all present, and everyone felt the presence of a suppressed Pentecost. An occasional cry or sob relieved a few hearts, and one young man, William Roberts, Clogwyn, actually shouted out a cry of despair; and when the preacher was at last able to pronounce the benediction, the congregation scattered without attempting the hymn which had been given out. The people walked home in groups, but spoke little to one another. A kind of awe now possessed

the whole of this part of the parish, and people talked of nothing on Monday but of the marvellous visitation of God.

It must now be remembered that though services were held at three different places in the parish, all the church fellowship meetings were held in Beddgelert. When the deacons, who had been waiting at the chapel-house for the hour of the fellowship meeting to arrive, saw a chapel full of people gathered together, they thought that someone must have spread a false rumour, and that they were expecting a preacher. How great was their surprise to find them all presenting themselves for membership . . .

The meetings now became very demonstrative, and the people shouted and leapt for joy. The hills rang with the hymns and hallelujahs as they journeyed to and fro. This glowing enthusiasm lasted until nearly every inhabitant of the parish had been stirred, and about two hundred had joined the church for the first time. Ministers from all parts of Wales became eager to witness the revival, and each one helped to fan the flame, and carried with him to other districts a spiritual aroma as delicious as the fragrance of unfolding foliage in spring . . . [1]

This revival had a mysterious precursor, or accompanying feature, known as 'music in the air'. It has been described as an indefinably sweet harmony, produced by a myriad angelic voices, which blended together in the softest tones. There was no distinct melody, but the music pinned each hearer to the spot on which he stood, as if all power of motion had left him. Scores have recorded their testimonies of having heard this music, and each one speaks of it as something which defies every definition.[2]

This remarkable movement of God in 1817, usually known

as 'the Beddgelert Revival', was particularly effective, Jenkins continues,

> in driving men to the Bible, and to show them its value as a pathway to their God. This resulted in the establishing of Sunday schools more generally, and in an earnest desire to revive the simplicity of worship which was characteristic of apostolic times.[3]

Other such revivals were to follow, each one making a significant impression upon a particular aspect of chapel life. One in 1832 stirred the people to their responsibility of teaching Christian truth to the young. Another, in 1859, swept right across Wales, driving the whole country to its knees, emphasising the great importance of prayer. In 1886, it was the value of Christian fellowship that was impressed upon the churches, as they were taught that success in God's work depended not upon the exceptional talents of a few but rather on the sincere commitment of every true believer. Yet all of these periods of religious awakening shared one overriding feature in common. Christian ministers preached the truth of God's Word with exceptional power, and many hundreds, of all ages, being made aware of their sin by God's Spirit, sought and found forgiveness and new life in God's Son, the Lord Jesus Christ. Further effects of these remarkable times of spiritual blessing, both social and spiritual, will be observed as the walk progresses, but we must press on.

From midway along the southern shore of Llyn Gwynant a gate gives access to a farm track which zigzags upwards through mixed woodland. Crossing a field, the path becomes rather indistinct and then plunges into a dense forest of tangled rhododendron. For a few days in the year when these shrubs are in bloom they are a picture. During the rest of the year, however, they represent a serious problem. For the farmer, their toxic leaves threaten to poison his sheep. For the ecologist, this non-indigenous plant introduced from the Himalayas spreads rapidly, depriving native species of both space and nutrients. Those who simply wish to follow a pathway across hillside or through woodland where these plants have taken hold soon discover that, unless they are regularly cut back, they can quickly obliterate any trail and render progress impossible. Fortunately, on this particular walk a clearer track is soon joined, which leads south-south-west through a conifer plantation before emerging across open pasture to join the Nanmor road (GR637494).

By this time I was very wet, not so much from falling rain as from the dense foliage through which I had necessarily to force my way. In actual fact it had now stopped raining, and for the first time that day the sky appeared to be getting brighter. I removed my waterproofs and ate some lunch before starting up the path that climbs steadily beside the stream flowing down from Llyn Llagi into Blaen Nanmor. Once level with the lake, this track takes an easterly course to the top of a sloping gully, where it turns due south and ascends steeply amongst boulders and heather to emerge on the northern shore of Llyn yr Adar. On a warm summer's day, the waterfall from the upper to the lower of these two lakes makes an interesting and refreshing scramble. But not today. Far too much water was pouring down Craig Llyn Llagi for me even to contemplate taking such a route.

I was now well beyond Llynnau'r Cŵn where I had planned to camp, but since it was only three-thirty in the afternoon I pressed on to cross the ridge which extends north-eastward from Cnicht and gives access to Cwmcorsiog. This is an area I know well but of which I never tire. Cnicht, though little more than 2250 feet high, is one of my favourite mountains.

Its long narrow ridge, and also the glorious prospects that open up as you follow it to the summit cairn, both combine to give this hill a majesty which some of its higher rivals possibly lack.

I was now moving downhill and quickly passed Llyn Cwmcorsiog on my left. This was very familiar territory, and with little more than four miles to cover I even began to consider the possibility of reaching the comfort of my home a day earlier than planned. However, the derelict buildings of the Rhosydd quarry were still half a mile away when a broad bank of storm cloud came sweeping in from the south-west. There may have been only four miles to go, but they would have been very wet miles, and the thought of a second soaking that day held little attraction. I had just reached a place where a small waterfall cascades down a low cliff from Llyn Clogwyn Brith (GR664466). Beside the stream there is a level area of firm grass. I had stopped here for lunch when walking with a friend a year before and had thought then how pleasant a spot this would be to camp. I hurried to erect the tent before the rain reached me and dragged my rucksack in behind me as the first heavy drops began to fall. The decision taken had been the right one. It rained steadily all evening. I was warm and dry, however, and enjoyed a generous portion of pasta before settling down for the night. If I rose early next morning I could be home before most of my neighbours had finished their breakfast, and have a day in which to rest and be refreshed.

Distance walked: 8 miles. (Total 28 miles.)

1   D. E. Jenkins, *Beddgelert, Its facts, fairies and folk-lore*. First edition (1899), pp. 364,5.

2   ibid., pp. 366,7.

3   ibid., p. 370.

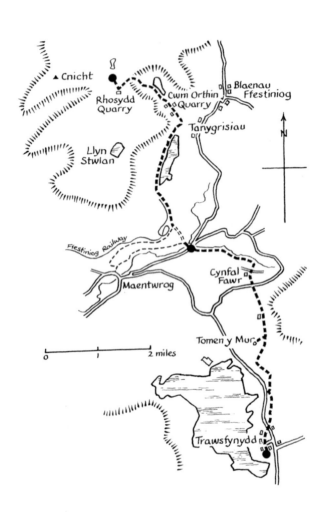

Cnicht

Rhosydd
Quarry

Cwm Orthin
Quarry

Blaenau
Ffestiniog

Tanygrisiau

Llyn
Stwlan

Ffestiniog Railway

Maentwrog

Cynfal
Fawr

Tomen y Mur

Trawsfynydd

N

0   1   2 miles

4
Cwm Orthin

I was woken by the flapping of the tent in a rising wind. Then the rain, which had eased during the night, began to fall again. I looked at my watch. It was just four o'clock, but the sky was already beginning to lighten. I lay there going over in my mind the ground I had covered in the previous three days. The weather thus far had not been particularly favourable, but this was Wales, I told myself, and heavy or continuous rainfall is not too uncommon. Furthermore, I had made good progress and was feeling fitter by the day, so I had no reason to feel hard-done-by.

In my mind I dwelt for a while upon Christian, the principal character in John Bunyan's *Pilgrim's Progress*. I thought of the heavy burden that he carried until he reached the place of the cross; of his struggle in the 'Slough of Despond' and the steep ascent of the hill 'Difficulty' after refreshing himself by a spring. Above all, I imagined his profound enjoyment of the 'Delectable Mountains' of which the shepherds spoke so warmly: 'These mountains are "Emmanuel's Land" and they are within sight of his City; and the sheep also are his, and he laid down his life for them.' After only three days I could already identify with so much of what Bunyan wrote. I thanked God not just for the privilege of being able to undertake this journey, but much more for calling me in his grace to walk life's pathway with him—a spiritual pilgrimage for which he equips his people, providing for them so thoroughly.

Realising by now that I was unlikely to sleep further, I ate a light breakfast and, with the rain easing slightly, packed up and prepared to move on. As I walked down toward the ruined buildings of Rhosydd Quarry a meadow pipit, feigning injury, fluttered along the ground in front of me dragging one wing. It clearly had a nest nearby, and was employing this tactic to lead what it considered a threat away from the vicinity of its young.

I have grieved previously[1] over the decline and dereliction of these quarry workings and the eyesore they now represent, so will not repeat my thoughts on the subject here. As I reached Rhosydd and turned eastward down into Cwm Orthin, however, the effects of spiritual revival upon the area once more came to mind. The religious awakening of 1859 was first seen in these parts among the men who laboured for slate in these very quarries. One eyewitness, writing in November 1859, describes the arrival of two men from Betws-y-coed who came seeking employment as quarrymen. They were already deeply troubled by a sense of guilt before God, and their weeping during the day did not go unnoticed by their fellow workers. The following day they were seen making their way to the top of the hill and were immediately followed by the entire workforce—in total about five hundred men. The record states:

> they halted on the summit of the mountain, and on that spot, under the broad canopy of heaven, they held a prayer meeting. While they prayed, the Holy Spirit was poured out upon them most abundantly. Nearly all present wept and sobbed aloud. On the same evening they met at their respective places of worship to pray. On the following day they met again on the mountain, leaving their work unheeded; for by this time the people were in a state of great religious excitement. The rocks seemed to re-echo

42

the voice of prayer and praise. On the following Saturday those who lived at a distance went to their homes, carrying with them the newly-kindled revival fire, and on the morrow the surrounding churches and chapels were in a blaze![2]

When reading such an account it should be remembered that those whose behaviour is thus described were tough, hard-living quarrymen. Drunkenness and violence were rife, both in the workplace and the home. Although nominally linked with a church or chapel, few of these men would regularly have attended a place of worship. Clearly something remarkable was happening. A powerful spiritual force was surely at work.

Walking through the rain towards Tanygrisiau, I was able to look down the Vale of Ffestiniog towards Maentwrog. The same local observer who detailed events in the quarry recorded the effect of the revival upon the young people of this village:

I do not believe that there was a worse place than the village of Maentwrog for its size within the principality. It was notorious for drunkenness and revelry, Sabbath-breaking and swearing, etc. You could hear the school children in passing, when playing together, using the foul language learnt of their parents at home, and that often with oaths and curses; but now these children hold prayer-meetings together. Where there is a group of houses, they assemble at one of them, and hold meetings at which they read, sing and pray together, sometimes for hours. Young men, from fifteen to twenty years old, are full of fire; they often meet to pray together in private houses after the public prayer-meeting is over, and continue to pray often till midnight, and sometimes till three and four o'clock in the morning.[3]

I make no apology for dwelling on this subject at some length and for quoting fairly extensively those who observed these events firsthand. Whether such scenes will ever be seen again, only God knows. As one, however, who shares the deep concern of many at the materialism, immorality and ungodliness of our own generation, one cannot help but yearn and pray for God to bring our nation back to himself in a mighty way.

The path I now followed passed the power station built on the western shore of Tanygrisiau Reservoir. This is one of two such pump-storage hydroelectric schemes found in north Wales. At off-peak periods electricity is used to pump water from this reservoir up to Llyn Stwlan, an artificial lake created by the construction of a large and unsightly dam 850 feet higher up in the shadow of Moelwyn Mawr. Then, when the national grid requires extra power, the water is allowed to flow back down to drive generators in the power station. Such generation of electricity may claim to be pollution-free, but it is virtually impossible to avoid major disfiguration of the natural landscape when such engineering work takes place.

One mile south of the reservoir, Dduallt on the Ffestiniog Railway is reached. There are those who see this railway line as a further despoiling of the countryside, especially at Dduallt where the track doubles back on itself in a 360 degree loop in order to gain height. For me, however, this is certainly not the gimmicky tourist attraction some would consider it to be. When it was built in 1836 to carry slate from Blaenau Ffestiniog to Porthmadog, this railway was to revolutionise the life and economy of the entire area. It served the local community long before tourism was ever recognised as a viable industry. Indeed, our own children, now grown up, still recall using the *trên bach* between Penrhyndeudraeth and Porthmadog as their daily means of transport to and from school.

Those wishing to follow this section of the line on foot will find an attractive path running between Tan-y-bwlch and Tanygrisiau. Since my own route was to cross the A496 at Pont Tal-y-bont (GR687416), however, I had kindly been given permission to walk through private land down to Plas Dol-y-moch. Here I met Chris, who served on the staff of this outdoor pursuit centre, and he kindly offered to drive me to my home further down the valley.

I would return tomorrow to resume my journey. It was only nine o'clock in the morning, but, wet and bedraggled, I was more than ready for a bath, breakfast and a well-earned rest.

Distance walked: 4 miles. (Total 32 miles.)

---

1   Mike Perrin, *Upon High Places,* Bryntirion Press (1997), pp. 69-73.
2   Thomas Phillips, *The Welsh Revival* (First published 1860; reprinted by Banner of Truth Trust 1989 and 1995), pp. 47-8.
3   ibid., p.52.

5
Cynfal Fawr and
Tomen-y-mur

By setting out from Llanfairfechan on a Wednesday, I had reasoned that it would not only be possible to spend Saturday night in my own home, but I would be able to attend the morning service in my own church on Sunday. Thankfully, this had proved possible, and so I resumed my journey at the point I had reached the day before, somewhat later than usual, but certainly much refreshed in body, mind and spirit.

My route left the A496 at Pont Tal-y-bont (GR687416). There is little to tell motorists travelling this road between Porthmadog and Blaenau Ffestiniog that they are actually crossing a bridge at this point, and few local people seem to know it by name. Viewed from the Cynfal gorge spanned by the bridge, however, one is at once impressed by both its size and its structure. The civil engineers who built this bridge and others like it certainly knew what they were doing, and built them to last.

Two paths lead eastward, clinging to the steeply wooded sides of the ravine. That on the north soon climbs steeply out of the gorge and crosses open fields toward Llan Ffestiniog, whilst the one on the south ascends more gradually, giving frequent glimpses of the foaming torrent below. It was the path on the south side that I took that pleasant afternoon. Above the constant murmur of the river, chiffchaff, willow warbler and cuckoo celebrated in song their recent safe arrival from far-off lands. Sunlight filtered through the fresh green canopy of native oak and ash. Bluebells and celandine carpeted the steep slope both below and above me, filling the air with a heady scent. Soon I arrived above the Rhaeadr Cynfal falls. From the footbridge which crosses the river at this point (GR705412), it is possible to see downstream a column of rock rising from the centre of the river. This is Hugh Llwyd's Pulpit.

Hugh Llwyd lived nearby in Cynfal Fawr during the reign of James I (1603–25). His reputation and claim to fame were probably eclipsed by those of his better known and more illustrious grandson, Morgan Llwyd. One suspects that Hugh also suffered from a bad press. He belonged to the gentry; he was a soldier who had seen action in Holland, and was known for his skill both as a huntsman and a poet. But he was also a physician and dispenser of herbal remedies, which in the sixteenth and seventeenth centuries was not always easily distinguishable from wizardry and the black arts. Was Hugh a magician or actively involved in witchcraft? Some clearly thought so, and believed his 'pulpit' to be the place to which he was accustomed to retire in order to commune with the devil. Others more kindly disposed towards him saw him as a relatively harmless mystic or spiritual man, who resorted to such a spot to meditate and pray. Clearly all manner of fanciful legends have been handed down concerning Hugh Llwyd and the significance of his rock in the middle of Rhaeadr Cynfal. The truth, however, is now unlikely ever to be known. Those who would seek for some tangible sign of Hugh's skill will find it at Cynfal Fawr itself.

Immediately above the footbridge the path turns sharply to the right and climbs in a southerly direction to join a minor road (GR704408). On the opposite side of the road a gated track leads up to the house. When I visited, it was unoccupied, but I was grateful to Gwilym and Anita Ephraim, the owners, for showing me around. They clearly take their custodianship very seriously and have long-term plans to restore the building to as near its original appearance as possible. Like so many old dwellings, it was 'modernised' in the 1960s with little attempt to preserve its unique architectural features. The building is composed of two parts: the old house, which has an impressive Elizabethan ceiling but probably predates this period; and a much larger dwelling, which was added in 1625 by Hugh Llwyd himself, with Gothic windows looking out towards Llan Ffestiniog and the Moelwyns beyond.

A slate plaque mounted on the wall of the old house states that Cynfal Fawr was also the birthplace and home of Morgan Llwyd (1619–59). Morgan was Hugh's grandson. At the age of fifteen he was sent to be educated at Wrexham. It was here that he came under the powerful influence of Walter Cradock's preaching. Cradock was already well known as one whose remarkable ministry had filled his church to overflowing and emptied the public houses of the town! It was not long before Morgan was converted, and a close friendship was forged between the two men. Indeed, Morgan was determined to follow in Cradock's footsteps and enter the Christian ministry. When Walter Cradock moved south to Brampton Bryan, near Knighton, Morgan served as a private chaplain to Sir John Harley, the Puritan squire there. He later assisted Cradock in establishing the very first nonconformist church in Wales, at Llanfaches in the Usk valley, in 1639. He returned to Wrexham in 1647, preaching not just in the town but travelling extensively across north Wales. Setting up several independent churches, including one that met in Cynfal itself, he was soon acknowledged as the father of Congregationalism in Meirionnydd.

Though he would later be acknowledged as one of the great Welsh Puritans, Morgan Llwyd ably demonstrated that these men highly esteemed for their deep theology and devotion to God were not lacking in wit, humour or an ability to appreciate and enjoy good things, as some have supposed. He was, in fact a discerning judge of well-bred horses and derived much pleasure from riding them. One day when in the saddle he met a justice of the peace travelling in the company of a lawyer. 'How is it that you, a lowly servant of God, can sit astride a fine horse when your Master saw fit to ride upon an ass?' asked the justice. 'Quite simply.' replied Morgan. 'Since my Master appears to have converted so many asses into justices, it has become well nigh impossible to purchase one at any price!' He died in 1659, the very same year as his great friend and fellow Puritan, Walter Cradock.

They were thus both spared the pain and persecution that followed the passing of the Act of Uniformity in 1662. This bill demanded the complete acceptance of the Anglican Prayer Book, and effectively outlawed the activity and preaching of anyone who was not ordained and licensed by the Church of England—something that was clearly unacceptable to those who had dissociated themselves from the Established Church and embraced nonconformity. (John Bunyan was imprisoned in Bedford jail for twelve years under this Act.) It would appear that unauthorised Christian meetings and the preaching of God's Word, prohibited by this legislation, continued at Cynfal even during this dark period. Morgan may have died, but his mother, Mari Llwyd, encouraged local Christians to meet in her home in spite of the dangers involved. Hugh Owen, of Bronclydwr near Tywyn, who had pastoral charge of all the Congregational churches in Meirionnydd, was a frequent preacher at Cynfal. Eventually Mari's faith and courage were rewarded, when she was able to have the building formally registered as a place of worship during an amnesty called by Charles II in 1672. Reluctantly I left this historic old building, deeply moved by all that it represented and had witnessed almost four centuries before.

The path now continues through the archway under the railway line. Once linking Blaenau Ffestiniog to Bala, this line closed when the Tryweryn valley was flooded by the waters of Llyn Celyn. A short section of track was left so that fuel rods and equipment could be moved more easily to and from the nuclear power station at Trawsfynydd, but since that in turn closed in 1992, no trains have passed this way.

Crossing the field beyond the railway line, a ewe lay on its back, unable to roll out of the shallow depression of the foot-path into which it had fallen. A distressed lamb bleated help-lessly by her side. By now too weak to struggle, and with tongue lolling from the side of her mouth, I thought at first she was already dead. As I rolled the sheep over, however, she feebly tried to struggle to her feet, only to collapse in a heap. I let her rest for a few minutes before taking hold of her thick fleece and lifting her upright once more. This time she stood by herself. Confident that she would now be all right, I walked on, to be closely followed by both ewe and lamb, each bleat-ing their gratitude. The three of us must have presented a strange picture indeed, but I shall admit to a feeling of warm satisfaction, having arrived at the scene of a potential tragedy in the nick of time!

South of the A470 the path continues to climb to nearly 1000 feet before reaching Sychnant farm, beyond which it enters a young conifer plantation and leads to Tomen-y-mur. This area is well worth taking some time to explore. Meaning 'Mound of the Wall', this ancient settlement sprang up at the junction of two Roman roads. The Sarn Helen came from the north-east and then continued southwards towards Dolgellau, crossing the A470 at Ganllwyd. At Tomen-y-mur, however, this key route was crossed by another road that ran between

Caer-gai, a fort near Bala, and the important Roman settlement of Segontium at Caernarfon. This would therefore have been an important crossroads from the first century onward. Serving both military and commercial needs, it almost certainly allowed the Christian message to reach these parts four hundred years before Augustine, sent by Pope Gregory I in AD 596 (and considered by some churchmen to be the bringer of Christianity to Britain), ever landed in Kent.

The clearly visible earthen banks and ditch that enclosed the fort were built in AD 78, although the mound at the centre is a Norman motte and was built in approximately AD 1095 by William Rufus, son and successor to William the Conqueror. As well as the fort, it is possible to trace the remains of a small amphitheatre, a square parade ground and a bathhouse, all relics of Roman occupation. The fort was abandoned around AD 140. One wonders what the native inhabitants made of it all, when the Romans left such an elaborate complex after only sixty years. Their sentiments were probably not very different from those expressed by their descendants of more recent days, when the power station just a mile away was closed by the Central Electricity Generating Board after an active life of only half that time!

From Tomen-y-mur my route led firstly south, then south-west beneath electricity power lines, before turning to the left on to a green road which descends to meet the main road (GR708372). It is possible to follow a footpath due south from this point, to emerge directly opposite the road leading up into Trawsfynydd village. I wanted to reach the village as quickly as possible, however, and so chose to walk along the side of the main road. Within five minutes I wished I had stayed on the footpath. As a car passed me at high speed, something small impacted with the windscreen and a leaf-like object dropped at my feet. I picked it up and held in the palm of my hand the lifeless form of a chiffchaff. I marvelled at the delicacy of its thin bill, the fragile beauty of its wings, and its bright but now unseeing eyes. I also felt an intense sadness— a sadness soon mingled with rising anger, that something created by God with such perfection and grace should be destroyed in an instant, sacrificed on the altar of man's insatiable need of speed and power. I drew some comfort from the words of Jesus, 'Are not two sparrows sold for a copper coin? And not one of them falls to the ground apart from your Father's will' (Matthew 10:29, New King James Version).

This six-mile leg of my journey is full of interest, yet not too demanding. Furthermore, its starting point at Pont Tal-y-bont and finish in Trawsfynydd village are both served by local bus routes (No.1 Caernarfon–Blaenau Ffestiniog, and No.2 Dolgellau–Porthmadog, respectively). A walk warmly recommended as an enjoyable day out for the family.

Distance walked: 6 miles. (Total 38 miles.)

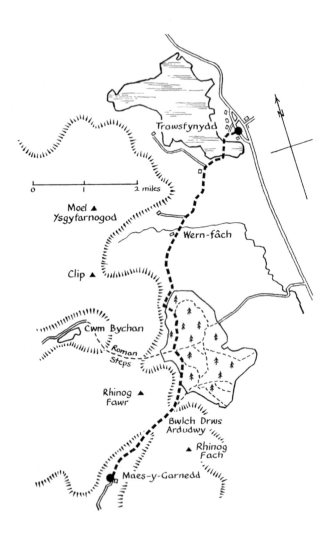

6
A wild day in
a wild place

I sat below the memorial to Hedd Wyn, map in one hand, a sandwich in the other. I was back in Trawsfynydd, with what I knew would be a demanding day ahead of me. The weather was by no means settled, and much of my route lay across trackless hillside with deep bog and dense heather. I looked up at the bronze figure above my head. Wearing gaiters and with sleeves rolled, he gazed resolutely toward the hills. They held no fear for him.

Ellis Humphrey Evans, born in 1887, had been a shepherd, and these hills and valleys were his home. The poetry he wrote echoed the great affection he had for these wild and lonely places. Even when Clip and Rhinog Fawr were wreathed in damp mist, he felt no anxiety. His *ffugenw*—the very name he had chosen and by which he desired to be known as a poet—reflected this, for Hedd means 'peace'. If anyone was truly at ease when cloud blanketed the mountains it was he.

Hedd Wyn was a son of Trawsfynydd, and some from this close-knit community would have been at the National Eisteddfod the year it was held in Birkenhead. According to custom, the winning poem was announced and Hedd Wyn was called forward to take the bardic chair. But there was no response from the gathered company. The year was 1917, and in that July Hedd Wyn had died in Flanders' fields.

I made my way through the outskirts of the village down to the walkway that has been built across the south-eastern corner of the lake. Developed in the 1930s, this stretch of water, over two miles in length, was intended to serve both as a reservoir and as a source of hydroelectric power. Today the huge concrete blocks that housed the water-cooled reactors of one of Britain's earliest power stations to use nuclear fuel dominate its northern shore.

Call me old-fashioned, but I have never been comfortable with the thought of such large quantities of highly radioactive material right on my own doorstep. I guess we all remember Chernobyl. Of course, my many friends who worked at the power station over the years all repeatedly told me how safe it was, and that what took place at Chernobyl 'could never happen here'. I could only hope they were right. Even so (and there is surely some irony in this), when the meltdown occurred at Chernobyl, and that vast cloud of radioactive dust drifted across Scandinavia, the North Sea and then the British Isles, it was heavy rain over Trawsfynydd that caused the surrounding hills to be so contaminated that the sheep are still scanned by Geiger counter to this day!

As I crossed the footbridge, such thoughts were far from my mind, however. A fresh breeze ruffled the surface of the lake, and clouds were gathering ominously in the north-west. Nevertheless, the first couple of miles were relatively straightforward, as I followed the metalled road south-west into Cwm Crawcwellt. I was heading for the shearing-sheds of Wern Fach (GR682332), only a short distance away; but it soon developed into a race as the hills to the north rapidly disappeared behind a grey curtain of advancing rain.

How thankful I was for those shearing-sheds! For forty minutes the rain drummed relentlessly on the corrugated-iron roof. Water gushed from the drainpipes to flow in rivulets across the enclosed gathering yard in front of the open-sided shed. Small puddles quickly became large pools. Then, driven on by the strengthening wind, as quickly as it had arrived the downpour ceased. My day's journey had barely begun and I was already behind schedule.

Without delay, therefore, I set off across the empty hillside. The Ordnance Survey 'Landranger' map made it look so simple. A clearly marked path ran south-west and then south to enter the forest at its northernmost edge. That is what the map indicates. Reality is somewhat different. What it all boils down to, I suspect, is that one man in a drawing office with ruler and pen (or possibly even a computer), and several hundred sheep on a Welsh hillside, have fundamentally differing views concerning what makes a good track! Not that I have anything against sheep-paths. I haven't. But they do have an annoying habit of either suddenly changing course or else disappearing altogether.

I soon abandoned any attempt either to find the footpath marked on the map or to follow sheep-tracks. Taking a compass bearing in case cloud and rain were to return, I set off to follow a fairly direct line across the cwm. Tussocky grass, interspersed with extensive patches of tall rush, made for slow progress. Then, as I approached the forest, it became particularly marshy. Large areas of sphagnum would move up and down disconcertingly below me as I tried to 'tiptoe' across. In such places it was possible to push my trekking-pole through the moss down as far as the handgrip without meeting any resistance. The thought of breaking through such a floating 'mattress' with the weight I was carrying was not something I wanted to dwell upon. As quickly as possible I endeavoured to gain firmer ground, and looked forward to reaching the forest, where hopefully conditions underfoot would improve.

Unfortunately, I was soon to discover that a high boundary fence had been erected, allowing no access whatsoever to the forest at that point, and it became necessary to follow the fence around under steep outcrops of rock until I eventually reached a stile at GR672312. A path (of sorts) followed a stream through the trees, emerging at last on a broad forest road. I felt a tremendous sense of relief and knew something of what David, the psalm-writer, meant when he celebrated God's mercy to him:

He lifted me out of the slimy pit, out of the mud and mire; he set my feet on a rock and gave me a firm place to stand.
(Psalm 40:2)

From this point onward the way became decidedly easier. At GR672297 a narrow track struck off to the right through young conifers, to emerge from the forest and join the main pathway across Bwlch Drws Ardudwy. The word *drws*, meaning 'a doorway', seemed most appropriate. The steep slopes of Rhinog Fawr to the north and Rhinog Fach to the south make this a particularly narrow portal, through which the wind, now up to gale force and blowing from the south-west, was funnelled with remarkable severity. I leaned into the wind and fought my way over the *bwlch* at a height of 1255 feet.

This is rugged and wild country. From Gellilydan in the north to Barmouth and Dolgellau in the south, this vast area, much of it well above 2000 feet, is scored by steep-sided gullies and covered by a mixture of tumbled boulders and tangled heather and bilberry. Hillsides rear up, not as grassy slopes but in rocky ledge upon rocky ledge. The highest summits of Rhinog Fawr and Rhinog Fach lack any obviously marked route to the top, whilst those brave and strong enough to tackle the classic traverse from Trawsfynydd to Barmouth, linking the summits of Moel Ysgyfarnogod, Clip, Rhinog Fawr and Rhinog Fach, y Llethr and Diffwys, face 23 miles of the toughest walking anywhere in Wales, involving in total 6250 feet of ascent!

Only three recognised paths cross this range in an east-west direction. One in the north between Trawsfynydd and Cwm Bychan passes immediately below Clip. Then the best-known of the three goes over Bwlch Tyddiad and also descends to Cwm Bychan by way of the Roman Steps (Roman by name, but more probably medieval in origin). And the third is the route I was following that day across Bwlch Drws Ardudwy down into Cwm Nantcol. Away from these paths the going is challenging indeed.

A group of seven friends, whose combined hill-walking experience was quite extensive, promised to spend a Saturday evening in our home after a day on the Rhinogs. They failed to arrive, which was a shame because they had promised to bring their own supper—and ours—from the local fish-and-chip shop! The telephone rang at nine o'clock the following morning. They had just descended to Cwm Bychan! Having seriously overestimated the distance they would be able to cover in a day's walking, they had been overtaken by darkness and had spent the night huddled together for warmth, and sheltering from the rain under an overhanging rock. Fortunately it had not been a cold night, and they were none the worse for their experience.

It is that kind of terrain. Strong ankles, reasonable lungs, and the ability to navigate accurately by map and compass, are the main prerequisites for exploring this rugged countryside. But the rewards are considerable.

I had not descended far before I met a rather confused and disorientated gentleman who told me he was looking for a Lancaster bomber that had crashed somewhere in the vicinity.

It is strange what tricks the mind plays on you when you are tired, but for some reason I at once thought of those bizarre reports of Japanese soldiers emerging from the Malayan jungle twenty years or so after the cessation of hostilities, not knowing that the war was over. Should I tell this gentleman that by now they had possibly located the wreckage? Clearly the exertion of the day was beginning to affect me.

It was not long before I reached Maesygarnedd farm at the head of Cwm Nantcol. This remote farmstead was once owned by the brother of Colonel John Jones, who married Oliver Cromwell's sister and lived here for a while. Colonel Jones was one of the signatories to the death warrant of Charles I. To distinguish him from all the other Joneses of the area he was therefore known locally as 'Jones the Regicide'. It is said of him that, becoming increasingly disillusioned with Cromwell's alleged failure to fulfil his promises, at the restitution of the monarchy he chose to give himself up to the Royalists. They very kindly allowed him to return to Wales to set his affairs in order before taking him to London, where he was hung, drawn and quartered!

By now it was late afternoon, and I was anxious to find a place out of the wind where I could camp for the night. Mr Evans, who now farms Maesygarnedd, kindly directed me to a nicely sheltered and dry place behind a solidly built stone wall. The wind continued to roar overhead like an express train, while in the lee of the wall the flysheet of the tent hardly stirred.

As I prepared my evening meal, above the noise of the wind I heard what I took to be a clash of arms. Did Colonel Jones still frequent this remote cwm? I looked out of the tent to see, just thirty yards away, a herd of eight wild goats. Two males with horns locked in combat were furiously fighting for the hand (or hoof) of one of the females!

I had only covered eight miles that day. It felt more like eighteen! Hopefully, by tomorrow the wind would have dropped. In the meantime, I was grateful to God that for now I was dry, well-fed, and sheltered from the ferocity of the wind. A peaceful night's rest was in prospect.

Distance walked: 8 miles. (Total 46 miles.)

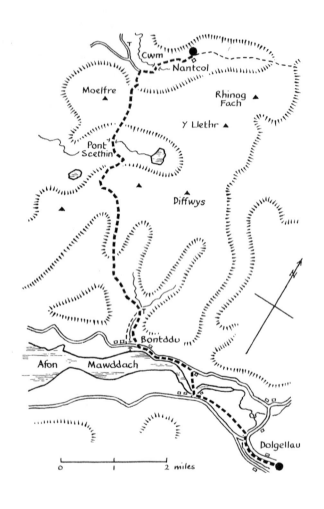

Cwm

Nantcol

Moelfre ▲

Rhinog
Fach ▲

Y Llethr ▲

Pont
Scethin

▲

▲

Diffwys ▲

▲

T

Bontddu

Afon Mawddach

Dolgellau

0   1   2 miles

7

Drystone-wallers
and golden nuggets

The strong wind had moderated during the night. I awoke from a good night's sleep feeling refreshed. Porridge, raisins and dried banana had been soaking overnight and required only a couple of minutes' simmering on the stove before breakfast was ready—and all before I ever emerged from the downy warmth of my sleeping bag. There are certain delightful aspects of lightweight camping that are virtually impossible to replicate at home!

By eight o'clock I was packed and ready to start. Nobody had yet emerged from the farm, but more than a hundred sheep and lambs came down from the lower slopes and followed me along the road. It would be nice to think that they were related to the one I had rescued near Cynfal Fawr, and were greeting me to express their appreciation. A more likely explanation is that they were hungry and thought I might be bringing them something other than grass to eat.

I intended to follow the narrow, delightfully winding road down Cwm Nantcol to a point just west of Cilcychwyn farm (GR631258), where a rather indistinct but waymarked track climbs in a southerly direction across the lower flank of Moelfre. Before starting the ascent, however, I hid my rucksack behind the wall and continued along the lane for another half a mile to a telephone box. Walking alone through remote countryside obviously carries some risk, and I had promised

Elaine that I would telephone her whenever possible. I have often been asked why I don't carry a mobile phone when walking alone in the hills. My first answer is that whenever I have met someone on top of a mountain speaking on a telephone, I have always found it quite incongruous and totally out of tune with the spirit of the hills. Surely, we go to remote places to get away from such things. The second is a more practical consideration. Unless one is on the very top of a mountain, the likelihood of getting a strong enough signal is very small. Indeed, it is not even guaranteed on a summit. This immediately puts anyone waiting to receive a call in something of a quandary. If an expected phone call fails to materialise, has the walker met with a serious accident, or are they simply out of range? How good it is to be able to enjoy unbroken communion with God when walking on the hills, without having to be concerned about strength of signal or the amount of power remaining in a battery!

Reaching the phone and dialling my home number, I heard my own voice on the answer machine. It told me that regrettably I wasn't there to take the call, but if I wished to leave a message after the tone they (or should it be I?) would get back to me . . . I actually did leave a brief message telling my wife that all was well, and returned to where I had left my rucksack.

For much of this first climb of the day the track ascends beside a stream, before eventually emerging on the *bwlch* between Moelfre and y Llethr at an altitude of 1400 feet. With the cloud base down to below 1500 feet, the view was restricted to whatever lay below me—and where Cwm Ysgethin is concerned, especially on an overcast day with drizzle, that is not very much. Apart from two lakes—Llyn Bodlyn, nestling below the slopes of Crib y Rhiw and Diffwys at the head of the cwm, and the smaller Llyn Irddyn on the opposite side of the valley—this appears to be a rather featureless and uninteresting

Llanfairfechan seashore—the start of the journey.

Nant Gwynant. The route lay along the left-hand shore of the lake before ascending the hillside through the visible breaks in the trees. Hafod Lwyfog nestles in the trees to the left of the picture immediately before Llyn Gwynant, whilst Hafod y Llan is hidden by the small hill at the far end (ch. 3).

From left to right, the Glyders (in the distance), Cnicht, Moelwyn Mawr and Moelwyn Bach, viewed from Porthmadog embankment. The route, whilst not traversing all of the summits, more or less followed the skyline (chs. 2, 3 and 4).

The derelict quarry chapel in Cwm Orthin, scene of a great religious revival in 1859 (ch. 4).

The parlour at Cynfal Fawr, home of Morgan Llwyd (ch. 5).

Pont Scethin which carried the stage coach across the Ysgethin river on its way from Harlech to London (ch. 7).

Crossing the Mawddach at Penmaenpool between Barmouth and Dolgellau (ch. 7).

The church of Llanfihangel-y-Pennant attended by Mary Jones (ch. 8).

part of Snowdonia. Without woodland (apart from some struggling conifers below Moelfre) or soaring crag to enliven the
landscape, it has a rather nondescript air. As I descended
toward Pont Scethin, however, I knew that I was surrounded
by history, reaching back in time over many thousands of
years. Wherever I looked on the map, there in Gothic lettering
was evidence of an ancient people who once occupied this
now empty cwm—*cairn, standing stone, settlement, homestead, burial chamber.* Who precisely were responsible for
these half-buried relics of a bygone age, and when did they
live here? Most of these remains date from Megalithic times
when, more than two thousand years before Christ, adventurers
from Spain, Portugal and Brittany began to colonise this
coastal strip of north-west Wales before gradually moving further inland. Some five hundred years BC, at the commence-
ment of the Iron Age, the first of the Celts settled in the vicinity,
the glory of battles fought and won celebrated by their bards.
They also left their mark on the landscape, with monuments like
Cerrig Arthur crossing the boundary between history and legend.

Not that there was anything legendary about Pont Scethin.
This delightful stone bridge (GR634235) is in as good condition now as the day it was built. This is one of my favourite
places,[1] and although it was raining I thoroughly enjoyed a
break for some food beside the stream, sheltered by the fern-
draped arch. In its heyday this little bridge was as important as
any river crossing on the A5 today, for it lay on the stagecoach
route between Harlech and London. I have often tried to picture the horses straining and the coach lurching and swaying
over the steep arch of the bridge. How I admired the men who
undertook such journeys! Drovers, too, would pass this way
with their herds on a 250-mile journey from Anglesey and the
Lleyn Peninsula to Smithfield market in London. Holding-pens,
where the cattle would be kept overnight, are still recognisable

a little way down the valley. But such journeys were not without danger, of course. The passage of wealthy travellers along this key route offered rich pickings for the criminally minded members of society. The ruined building below Moelfre (Tynewydd on the OS map) was once an inn and the frequent haunt of highwaymen and robber bands, who would lie in wait for the stagecoach or cattlemen returning from London with the proceeds of their business.

Thankfully, no such danger threatened me as I began the zigzag climb up and over Llawllech. Only the encouragement which came from a touching inscription on a slate memorial stone by the side of the path:

To the enduring memory of
JANET HAIGH
who even as late as
her eighty-fourth year
despite dim sight
and stiffened joints
still loved to walk this way
from Talybont to Penmaenpool

. . . .

Courage, traveller!

The stone had been placed there by her son Mervyn, Bishop of Winchester, after her death in 1953. She must have been quite a lady, I thought, and I wondered whether I would be able to undertake the same journey myself in another twenty years time!

I was to meet some equally remarkable characters for myself very shortly. The route taken by the stagecoach, and which I was also following that morning, crosses the ridge at a height of 1835 feet, before it begins its descent to Bont-ddu. Along the crest of the ridge, for a distance of approximately seven miles, from y Llethr in the north to Barmouth in the south, runs a six-foot-high drystone boundary wall. Low cloud reduced visibility to about twenty yards and it was raining steadily as I approached the gate. It was then that I saw two men working. Father and son, with apparent disregard for the weather, were rebuilding the wall. They had walked up earlier that morning from their Landrover parked 1000 feet below, they told me. The father must have been approaching seventy years of age! I stood watching them for some time, marvelling at both their skill and their cheerfulness as we chatted and joked together. Scattered all around on the ground lay rocks of every shape and size. Yet without hesitation they would select just the right one, seeming to know instinctively exactly where it would fit. What craftsmanship! What commitment to a task so backbreaking and with, I suspected, little in the way of reward save the knowledge of a job well done! What determination, in spite of the absence of anyone, apart from myself, to appreciate and admire their handiwork! As I stood watching, I was reminded very much of the unseen patience and perseverance of God who, when confronted by a human life that has fallen apart and become chaotic, sets to and rebuilds it with such care and precision that it stands upright and endures to his praise and glory. How often had I experienced, even in my own life, God fitting just the right 'building stone' into its place, when I had no knowledge whatsoever of what needed to be done!

Feeling tremendously privileged to have met and talked with these men, and having learnt so much from watching them at work, I left them to their wall, the mist and the rain, and continued on my way. From the ridge, the coach road sweeps around the head of the cwm and descends the grassy shoulder of Braich (meaning 'an arm'), down toward the estuary. The view to the south across Afon Mawddach and Cadair

Idris is breathtaking. Not quite so enjoyable, however, was the steep, knee-jarring descent on tarmac, after the soft luxury of so much green road. At the phone box (GR667198), I therefore turned off to the right to follow a footpath alongside the river down to the main road.

Passing by a mine surrounded by impressive security fences, I remembered that I was in an area that had a history of gold-mining going back to pre-Roman times. One mine had only ceased working recently and could easily start up again if a buyer were to be found. The sun had now decided to shine, and I peered down into the water hoping to catch the glint of a gold nugget among the stones of the river bed! And yet that day I felt indescribably rich, even without such an exciting discovery. For a whole week now the hills had been mine to enjoy, free from interruption. Without the modern world's constant clamour for attention, and the rush and bustle, the noise and pollution associated with 'progress' on the eve of a new millennium, I had been able to bathe in the stillness and solitude of truly wild places. Creatures 'great and small' had watched my slow progress, even as I had observed theirs. The changing face of the weather had brought infinite variety to my journey, even though it was only a week old; while under my very feet, often unnoticed, another springtime had heralded a rich diversity of wild flowers of every hue.

I recalled a moment eight months before when I had been walking in the Alps. A friend and I had trekked right around the Mont Blanc massif, and we were crossing from Switzerland back into France at a height of some 6500 feet, when I noticed some tiny white flowers at the side of the path. I picked one and examined it through the magnifying lens of my compass. So engrossed was I that I failed to notice the approach of a stranger until he spoke. 'What have you found— a gold nugget?' he asked. Instinctively I replied, 'Yes, a gold nugget indeed.' The flower I was examining was not simply white, as I had at first thought. Under the magnifying glass the tips of the petals were veined with purple, while on the lower of its two lips shone a bright yellow spot. By this time the stranger was looking over my shoulder. 'Ah, *Euphrasia Salisburgensis*', he muttered. 'A member of the family of Eyebrights. Not particularly rare, but a gold nugget to be sure.' He introduced himself. He was a Dutch botanist and the author of a recently published work on alpine flora.

I felt so very grateful that in these ways God was allowing me to enjoy so many wonderful facets of his beautiful world and increasing my understanding of his ways. Rich indeed!

> The judgments of the Lord are true and righteous altogether,
> More to be desired are they than gold,
> Yea, than much fine gold;
> Sweeter also than honey and the honeycomb.
>
> (Psalm 19:9-10, New King James Version)

On arrival at Bont-ddu there is little option but to walk along the A496 to the Penmaenpool toll bridge and cross the estuary at that point. There was a wide enough verge, however, and with such views to the south who is going to notice the occasional car or lorry? The view from the bridge itself down-river is special, too, while on the other side of the Mawddach the Wildlife Information Centre is well worth a visit, before following the now disused railway line into Dolgellau.

Another day's walking successfully completed! By tomorrow I would have covered a third of the distance.

Distance covered: 10 miles. (Total 56 miles.)

---

1 Mike Perrin, *Upon High Places*, pp. 37-9.

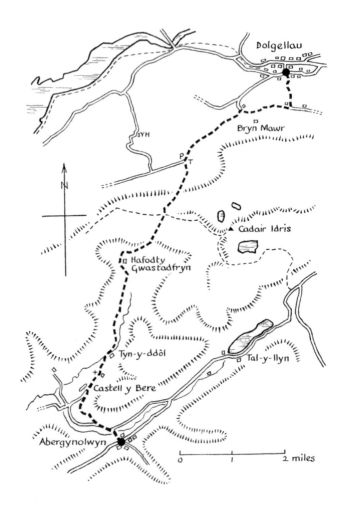

8
In Cadair's shadow

Whether viewed from the surrounding hills which hem it in on three sides, or from any one of its narrow, crooked streets, Dolgellau strikes one as being very much a product of the landscape in which it is located. A perfect example of town 'non-planning', its buildings of hard stone and smooth grey slate have evolved over many years, to reflect local geology and local craftsmanship.

There is no symmetry here. There are open places called 'squares' that are triangular. Streets meet one another at every conceivable angle except ninety degrees! Buildings constructed from rough-hewn rock at the beginning of the seventeenth century exist alongside the more stately dressed stone and Gothic-style windows of the mid-1800s. Yet there is harmony. Quaintness and elegance combine to please the eye and arouse curiosity as to what lies around the next corner.

We left Meyrick Square (or triangle!) under a blue sky that promised a bright, warm day—'we', because today was going to be pleasantly different. I was to have company. Phil Thomas and his wife Kate have been our friends for many years. A local resident and former geography teacher in the town, Phil now worked as a part-time warden for the Countryside Council for Wales in the Cadair Idris area. What better qualifications could I have in a travelling companion for today's walk over to Abergynolwyn? I was also travelling 'light', for I planned to return to Dolgellau by road that evening, to spend the night with my friends before continuing

71

south the following day. A most enjoyable walk was in prospect.

The lane leading south out of the town was soon exchanged for a pleasant tree-lined footpath that climbed steeply out of the valley. A lamb with its head caught in the mesh of a wire-netting fence provided an early diversion. Another rescue effected, we travelled on. Soon we were traversing a hillside above a wooded gorge. On the far side stood two remote dwellings, both of considerable antiquity.

Esgeiriau (GR729167) housed a family in the seventeenth century who were in the habit of holding Christian meetings in their home. The local church authorities were strongly opposed to such a practice, and incited a mob to attack the house. The occupants were forced to flee for their lives, whilst their furniture and belongings were carried from the house and hurled into the ravine.

Another family who were living close by in Bryn Mawr (GR728165) fared little better. Rowland Ellis, the head of the household, joined the Quaker movement in 1672. He was arrested, along with other members, for refusing to take the Oath of Allegiance to the king. Quakers believed that the swearing of any kind of oath was contrary to the teaching of Scripture; a belief which resulted in many being charged with treason or papal intrigue. Ellis and his fellow members were tried in Bala, where, along with their families, they faced a sentence of death. Mercifully, the judge was shown to be dispensing a law that had already been repealed, and the prisoners were released. After further persecution this family emigrated to Pennsylvania where, to this day, there is an educational establishment known as the Bryn Mawr Ladies College.

We soon joined the lane to the south of the town and turned west to reach Rhydwen. Turning left, a no less attractive road led past Llyn Gwernan to the car park and picnic site at GR698153. Seventy-five yards further on, a gateway on the left marks the beginning of the Pony Path. Not far from the road we paused by a memorial erected by the Cadair Idris Race Committee in memory of Will Ramsbotham. Every year, fell runners compete in a race from the town centre to the top of Cadair and back down again. On Saturday 5 June 1993 the race was won by Will, a member of Pudsey and Bramley Athletic Club, in a remarkable record time of 1 hour 25 minutes. Tragically, the glory of this amazing achievement was short-lived. The following day, whilst climbing on the Cyfrwy Arete of Cadair Idris, he fell to his death.

Earthly success and the glory that accompanies it can be tremendously rewarding while it lasts, but it can be fleeting also, and so quickly snatched away. To compete in a race of this kind is courageous: to win, a tremendous achievement. But to strive for a heavenly and lasting reward is to display the greatest wisdom of all. As Phil and I read the inscription on the memorial plaque, we thought of words written by the apostle Paul:

in a race . . . everyone who competes . . . goes into strict training . . . to get a crown that will not last. Run in such a way as to get the prize . . . a crown that will last for ever.
(1 Corinthians 9:24-25)

In a distance of just one mile, the Pony Path climbs over 1300 feet to a col (GR692135). Those making for Pen y Gadair, the highest point on Cadair Idris, will bear left at this point and follow the ridge high above Llyn y Gadair to the summit. Sadly, we had no time for such a detour, and carried on over the *bwlch* to begin the descent toward Llanfihangel-y-Pennant and the Dysynni valley.

As we started down, I was at once impressed by the sheer scale of the cwm we had entered. This huge basin was almost two and a half miles across from east to west, and we would need to walk a similar distance in a southerly direction before we reached the road. To the west, north and east, a continuous ridge between 2000 and 2900 feet high hemmed us in, interrupted only by the pass of Rhiw Gwredydd over which we had just come. We marvelled at the remoteness and isolation of this vast region. A recently constructed track, giving better access to the upper slopes in the west, was the only evidence of human activity we could see. To be designated as an SSSI (a Site of Special Scientific Interest) means that wild animals, birds and plants can hopefully thrive here with only minimal interference by man.

Yet, as we descended toward some largely overgrown and ruined buildings, we were reminded of a bygone age when, during the summer months at least, this remote cwm would have been inhabited. The name Hafoty Gwastadfryn (GR678122) indicated that this used to be a summer dwelling (Welsh: *hafod* or *hafoty*), where a family would have lived from spring through to the autumn, tending their flocks on these higher slopes. Similar high-level homesteads, occupied only in the summer, are to be found in other European mountain areas such as Switzerland. Today, at least as far as Welsh hills are concerned, 4 x 4 vehicles and quad-bikes have made such a practice unnecessary.

To young Mary Jones in 1800, however, such farmsteads would have been a welcome 'oasis' on her way to and from Bala. Mary lived in Tyn-y-ddôl (GR673095), a cottage whose ruined walls have now been partially rebuilt and enclose a stone memorial recording her well-known but none the less remarkable story. Living beside Afon Cadair, just half a mile north of Llanfihangel-y-Pennant, with only a couple of neighbouring farms for company, Mary's childhood must have been quite a lonely one. But in her early years she was made aware of God's grace and love for her in Christ, and devoted her youthful energy to discovering more about him.

When she was just ten years of age, a Sunday school opened in Abergynolwyn; here she was taught to read by John Ellis of Barmouth, and soon developed an appetite for the Word of God. Bibles were extremely scarce in those days, however, the nearest copy being in Penybryniau Mawr, a farmhouse two miles away from her home. Regularly Mary visited the farm, where she was allowed to read and memorise the Scriptures, all the while saving every penny she could earn for the day when she would be able to afford a Bible of her own.

One day, on her way to Penybryniau Mawr, she met a man on horseback who enquired concerning her business. It was the Revd Thomas Charles of Bala. Moved by Mary's devotion, he invited her to visit him in Bala, where he was shortly expecting a consignment of Welsh Bibles from London. The story of Mary's twenty-five-mile walk from Llanfihangel-y-Pennant to Bala, barefooted and with her precious savings and a little food in her satchel, has often been told. Indeed, it has passed into the annals of Christian history. Following a plea by Thomas Charles for more copies of the Bible in Welsh, at a meeting in London in which he narrated Mary's story, in 1804 the British and Foreign Bible Society was formed.

If so frequently told, therefore, why repeat the story once again? My answer is simple. As I walked the very paths she would have walked, and viewed the mountains she would have crossed with bare feet; as I considered how few of this world's possessions and comforts she would have had to enjoy, and thought of her great desire and determination to possess, above all else, a Bible of her own to read and benefit from—I was deeply challenged in my own heart and conscience. Mary's example leaves us all with this uncomfortable question: Precisely what value do we place on God's written Word? 'I love your commands more than gold, more than pure gold', said the psalmist, and his reason for saying this was expressed in this profound statement: 'Your word is a lamp to my feet and a light for my path' (Psalm 119:127,105). Sixteen-year-old Mary Jones felt the same. Do we?

Mary later married Thomas Lewis and moved to his home in Bryn-crug, near Tywyn (GR609034). There she was to spend the rest of her days, dying at the age of eighty and being buried in the graveyard of Bethlehem chapel in the village. A more detailed account of her life and love for Christ is to be found in *To Bala for a Bible* by Elisabeth Williams.[1]

As we resumed our journey, it was not long before we reached some more ruins. Above the lane, hidden among the trees on the top of a rocky outcrop, are the remains of Castell y Bere (GR667085). Built by Llywelyn Fawr in 1221, this was once considered to be among the most important of Welsh castles. Following the death of Llywelyn ap Gruffydd (Llywelyn the Last) near Builth in December 1282, it was at this castle that his brother Dafydd held out for four months under siege by the forces of Edward I. In April 1283 the castle fell. Dafydd was hunted down and put to death in October that year, thus bringing to a sad end the dynasty of native Welsh princes.

Turning left at the crossroads and following Afon Dysynni in a south-easterly direction, we soon reached the village of Abergynolwyn and the end of our day's ten-mile journey. Phil and I had shared much together: the exhilaration of a good walk through beautiful countryside; the recollection of days when being faithful to Christ frequently meant making great sacrifices; the moving account of triumph turning into tragedy—but, above all, the deeply challenging example of a sixteen-year-old girl who believed that finding God in his Word, the Bible, was the single most important thing in the whole world.

Distance walked: 10 miles. (Total 66 miles.)

---

1   Bryntirion Press (1988).

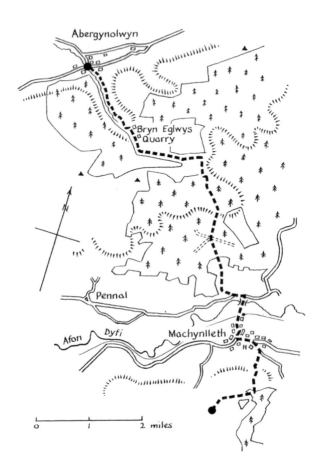

9
The Tarrens

The route south from Abergynolwyn is barred by a range of hills generally known as the Tarrens. Rising behind Tywyn in the west, this ridge runs for almost twelve miles over four distinct summits, reaching 2188 feet at its highest point, before dropping down to Corris in the east.

Located anywhere else in Snowdonia, this area would undoubtedly be far more popular than it appears to be. Overshadowed by its impressive neighbour, Cadair Idris, these little known hills on the southernmost border of the National Park attract comparatively few visitors, in spite of the delightful prospects they afford and the excellent walking they offer. I for one would welcome an opportunity to explore these mountains further. I have to admit, however, that on this particular morning I was venturing into completely new territory, as one whose previous knowledge of the area was embarrassingly small.

The narrow metalled quarry road that leads south-east from Pandy Square in the centre of the village comes as something of a shock to the system first thing in the morning. Those who, like me, prefer to 'warm up' gently to the exertion of the day will hardly welcome the way in which it immediately rears up in front of them. There was some consolation in the fact that I quickly gained height, however, whilst the views down into Nant Gwernol, or the Wild Ravine as it is sometimes called, went some way toward taking my mind off such effort at eight-thirty in the morning!

It is possible to turn off to the right on a footpath at the foot of the hill and follow the river to a bridge (GR686061). This gives access to a forestry road which loops south-westward before heading back east to the disused Bryn Eglwys quarry. The same height has to be climbed whichever route is taken, however, and with low cloud threatening rain I opted for the more direct route of the two. John Gillham's *Snowdonia to the Gower* guide became increasingly valuable as I made my way through the quarry. Many of the shafts and deep pits are potentially dangerous, and the path he recommends is not marked on the OS map. His instructions are very clear, however, and it is possible to pass through this complex of inclines and spoil tips, ruined buildings and collapsed chambers, both speedily and safely.

Leaving the quarry behind, the path climbed gradually in a south-easterly direction across occasionally marshy ground toward Foel y Geifr. At GR701049, Nant Gwernol turns to the east, and the river is crossed by an ancient packhorse bridge. Pont Llaeron is said to be of Roman origin—a claim which supports the argument for routing the Sarn Helen up Nant Gwernol and over the Tarrens to the Roman fort at Cefn-caer, near Pennal (GR704000). It has to be admitted that the more likely route from Dolgellau would have been by way of the Tal-y-llyn pass, crossing the A487 (GR762150) and continuing by way of Aberllefenni and Corris on to Machynlleth. Standing at Pont Llaeron beneath low cloud and in steady drizzle, however, one felt a sense of mystery in the air. Was that the sound of marching feet; the noise of armour against leather, or just the wind in the trees or water as it tumbled over the rocks?

The path continued up between the edge of the forest and the stream, climbing steadily until it reached the *bwlch* (GR718054). I only wish I could describe the glorious view southward across the valley of the Dyfi toward Pumlumon (or Plynlimon as some prefer). I would dearly have liked to see it myself, since I would be walking that way tomorrow. But alas, swirling cloud and a curtain of rain obscured all but the near-by conifers into which I would now have to plunge.

Crossing a stile into the plantation, the path began to descend around the rim of a deep cwm, Nant Lliwdy. The forest road follows a rather erratic course southward, and in several places yellow waymarking indicated 'short cuts'. However, given the neglected condition of these (the route also forms part of the Dyfi Valley Way at this point), it is doubtful whether following them saves any time. An imposing 'junction' where five ways meet is reached (GR729033), and a path heading south-east taken. Initially a forest trail, it soon leaves the shelter of the trees to become a very pleasant green road, before changing into the inevitable tarmac and joining the A493 three hundred yards west of the bridge over the river.

My feelings at crossing the Dyfi were similar to those I felt at the Penmaenpool bridge over Afon Mawddach, and to a lesser degree at Pont Dol-y-moch over Afon Dwyryd near Maentwrog. The geography of Wales is such that these rivers represent major boundaries between successive areas of upland. As each river was reached and crossed, therefore, I felt my progress being measured by these significant 'milestones' as I journeyed south.

As Welsh towns go, to describe Machynlleth as 'unusual' may be something of an understatement. Approaching from the north, one of the first things to attract my attention was a group of tipis (or 'wigwams' to the uninitiated) set back from the road near the railway station. This is the home of a company known as 'Shelters Unlimited', who specialise in the manufacture of these unusual but very attractive dwellings. I would say at this point that visitors to Machynlleth are likely to discern quite a strong New Age influence as they explore the town. Several shops display crystals, joss sticks, talismans and potions, not to mention all manner of books on astrology, magic and alternative therapies; whilst those manufacturing their tipis unquestionably have a particular interest in the tribal traditions and beliefs of the Native Americans.

Now, as a Christian, I am clearly unable to accept the basic philosophy underlying this movement which has become so popular in recent years, and especially the concept of pantheism which teaches that God is nature and nature is God. I firmly believe that there is a close link between God and nature, arising from the assumption that the former is the sole creator of the latter. 'In the beginning God created the heavens and the earth' are the words with which the Bible begins (Genesis 1:1), and the New Testament echoes that truth: 'he made the universe . . . sustaining all things by his powerful word' (Hebrews 1:2,3).

This, of course, places a great obligation upon me to care for the environment in which God has put me, and not to abuse it in any way. The universe round about does indeed 'declare the glory of God; the skies proclaim the work of his hands' (Psalm 19:1). But to equate the material world, be it a tree or an animal or a mountain, however magnificent in and of itself, with God, is something I can never do. I need a personal God with whom I can interact, one to whom I can talk and who is able to speak to me.

But at the same time, I am not going to dismiss or condemn the concern expressed by those who feel strongly about environmental issues. Nor will I forgo the pleasure of sleeping in a tipi, simply because of the philosophy of those who have championed such causes or popularised this form of dwelling. (Both of our sons have used tipis as extensions to their homes during the summer months, and great fun they are.)

As you enter the town, the sense of history is quite tangible. There was a settlement on this site as far back as the Iron Age, and the Romans certainly recognised the strategic significance of its position when they built a military base here. During the sixth century it became known as a rallying place from which attacks were launched against the Anglo-Saxon threat from the south and east.

Its greatest claim to historical fame, however, lies in the fact that it was this town that Owain Glyndwr chose as the capital of the country he had freed from the rule of Henry IV (1399–1413). His parliaments were assembled at various times in Dolgellau, Harlech and here at Machynlleth. Indeed, the Parliament House still stands, though much restored, in Stryd Maengwyn. But it was Machynlleth that witnessed his coronation in 1404—a fact that ensured that the town would forever be a symbol of Welsh pride and national spirit. This was a key factor, no doubt, in the minds of those who, in 1999, campaigned (albeit unsuccessfully) for Machynlleth to be made the home of the newly formed National Assembly of Wales.

It was lunchtime when I reached the town centre, and I had already walked eight miles that morning. There was time to look around and, most importantly, to eat. A wholefood café serving generous portions at modest prices was a most welcome discovery. I then visited Greenstiles, a shop retailing outdoor equipment, to collect one of the several food parcels I had sent in advance to await my arrival. Each parcel contained pre-packed portions of dry or dehydrated food sufficient for two days, and considerably lightened the load I needed to carry at any given time. I also enclosed the maps I would need on the next stage of my journey, together with a stamped and addressed envelope for the return of those that were no longer required.

Having walked all the way from Abergynolwyn without meeting a single person, it was nice to pass the time of day and chat with folk in a leisurely manner; to talk about the town and its surroundings—its past history and the modern problems facing the farming community in particular. I was struck by the friendliness of people and the unhurried pace of life, which allowed time to communicate even though we were meeting as strangers. In fact, it was not long before I was thinking of the very different 'welcome' given to another visitor to Machynlleth some two hundred and fifty years earlier. Howell Harris was one of the great preachers raised up by God during a period of spiritual revival in the eighteenth century. Much of his time and energy was devoted to travelling around Wales, speaking whenever an opportunity arose and wherever a company of people might be gathered. He visited Machynlleth around 1740. The following is a loose translation from Welsh written in his own words, describing the reception he was given:

When I came first to Machynlleth, I quickly realised that I was not welcome. However, I determined to preach by the roadside to whoever might listen. I found a suitable place and began to speak, but soon had to stop because of the noise of the crowd who shouted, threatened and swore, and because of the stones or whatever else came to hand, that they threw at me. One in particular, a lawyer, came to me with such hatred in his looks, and hellish language in his mouth, that his name might have been 'Legion'. With him were two others, an aristocrat and a priest, displaying the same temperament and language, inciting the common folk. One of them fired at me with a pistol without causing me hurt, but as I was surrounded by the crowd in the middle of the road, I thought that I should never escape from them alive, their attitude being such that they threatened me with death. But my hour had not yet come, and although I did receive rough treatment from them, I was strongly delivered from their hands. Eventually it was one of the rioters that sought my horse, but as soon as I had mounted they came again to meet me, and once more began pelting me with sticks and stones, until the Lord saved me out of their hands.[1]

Although he was received with such hostility on this occasion, it was not long before the town was to experience remarkable blessing from the hand of God, with many of the local people being brought to faith in Christ. This was not the first time that bitter persecution was followed by a period of spiritual awakening. Jesus certainly warned his followers that he was sending them out like lambs among wolves, but it is also recorded that he sent them ahead of himself to every town and place where he was about to go. Perhaps we have an example of this happening two and a half centuries ago in this now quiet and peaceful town of Machynlleth, once capital of Wales.

By mid-afternoon I was on my way again. Tomorrow would be a long day, so the further I could get that night, the better. Shortly after passing the Parliament House, a minor road forks right to Forge, and immediately after the cottage hospital, a footpath heads south across a golf course. The path soon climbs to give extensive views across the valley to the Tarrens and Cadair Idris beyond, before levelling off and passing through a short section of forest (GR756993). A family of Canada geese moved gracefully across the tranquil waters of Llyn Glanmeryn as I turned south-west and descended to Glanmeryn farm. Calling at the house, I sought permission to camp in the vicinity and was kindly directed to an area of woodland alongside a stream. It was not long before I was comfortably established and ready for a relaxing evening and peaceful night's sleep. I was not aware of strong winds during the night, but the next day I was to meet a fellow walker who had camped a mile further up the valley near Bwlch farm. He had slept little and suffered a broken tent pole because of the ferocity of the wind.

I fell asleep thinking of the courage and commitment of men like Howell Harris, who were prepared to risk life and limb in their determination to proclaim God's love in an embittered and hostile world. Oh for such men and women today!

Distance walked: 11 miles. (Total 77 miles.)

---

1   Rev. John Hughes (Liverpool), *Methodistiaeth Cymru, Cyfrol I*, R. Hughes a'i Fab (Wrexham, 1851), p. 99.

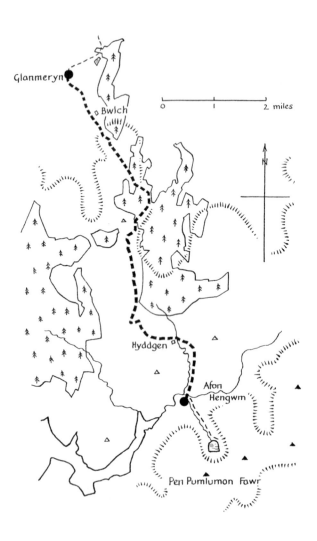

Glanmeryn

Bwlch

0   1   2 miles

N

Hyddgen

Afon
Hengwm

Pen Pumlumon Fawr

10
Hyddgen

I awoke from a good night's sleep with high expectations. The weather was fair and I was about to begin the eighteen-mile traverse of 2467-feet-high Pumlumon. Allowing two days so that I could really savour this lonely and comparatively unspoilt area, I planned to camp overnight somewhere near the summit. This was to be new territory for me.

Thirty years before, when I had been an active member of SARDA, I had been flown by RAF helicopter to this area with my dog Elsa. A party of schoolchildren had been on a field trip to the source of the River Wye, when two of their number decided to go 'absent without leave' and do some exploring on their own. They were found safe and sound (at least until their teacher caught up with them!), but I recall little of the incident or the terrain. Today, without the noise of helicopter engines or the responsibility of working a search and rescue dog, I could enjoy the beauty of this great expanse of wild mountain country.

Pumlumon (or Plynlimon as it is sometimes called) is really a broad ridge consisting of five summits, all over 2000 feet, from whose flanks flow five major rivers: the Severn, Wye, Rheidol, Ystwyth and Clywedog. One possible derivation of the name Pumlumon is from the two words *pump* (meaning 'five') and *llumon* (meaning 'beacon' or 'peak'). Viewed from the Aberystwyth road to the south, the region has been described as 'featureless'. Approaching by way of the ancient trackways from the north, however, the true character of the region can be fully appreciated. Silver ribbons of water cascade from the steep escarpment, to plunge into the hidden depths of afforested cwms. Secluded valleys separated by broad spurs of moorland extending north-westwards are surmounted by finely sculptured summits. From the summit cairn on Pumlumon Fawr on a clear day the whole sweep of Cardigan Bay is visible, from Bardsey Island to the rocky promontories of the Pembrokeshire coast. Snowdon to the north, the Wrekin in Shropshire, and the Black Mountains and Brecon Beacons in the south may all be identified.

Yet to extol the virtues of this broad and beautiful landscape without warning of its dangers would be grossly irresponsible. Those who walk these hills need to be aware of two things.

First, the area contains many hazardous peat-hags or moss pools of great depth. Largely hidden from view, the danger does not become apparent until one has broken through and is beginning to sink. Where there is no path, it is wisest to follow a stream, the bed of which is usually much firmer than the surrounding bog. Then, secondly, these uplands are frequently subject to mist that can form suddenly, even on a fine day, and quickly envelop an entire area. Navigation then becomes a real test of skill with map and compass. Indeed, for those whose ability in this realm may be questionable, the best advice might even be to find a sheltered spot and remain where you are. I was to become very aware of both these dangers a little later in the day.

I left Glanmeryn farm at about eight-thirty and began walking south-east towards Bwlch. Sitting for a while on a stile, I read Psalm 146:

Blessed is he whose help is the God of Jacob, whose hope is in the LORD his God, the Maker of heaven and earth, the sea, and everything in them—the LORD, who remains faithful for ever.

How good it is, when surrounded by such beauty, to be reminded of such things!

Beyond Bwlch the path climbed steadily, with extensive views south-west across the valley toward the waterfall of Pistyll-y-llan. The sun broke through shortly before I entered the forest at Rhiw Goch (GR767955). It was both dark and damp following yesterday's heavy rain, but here and there were small clearings where the sun's rays shone through and were turned into solid shafts of light by the mist rising from the moist forest floor.

Emerging from the forest, a substantial track contours above the cliffs of Creigiau Bwlch Hyddgen, with a glorious vista opening up this time toward the east. It was just below Foel Fras (1735 feet) that I met a fellow traveller named Mike. He told me of the wild night he had spent camping in a particularly exposed place, and of the way in which his tent pole had been broken by the strength of the wind. Unfortunately, this was not to be his only encounter with especially harsh elements that day.

We were both heading in the same direction, but he was tired and insisted that I went on ahead. Soon I was descending open moorland toward Nant Hyddgen. Quiet and peaceful now, it was once the scene of a momentous and bloody battle.

On 16 September 1400, at Glyndyfrdwy between Llangollen and Corwen, Owain Glyndwr was declared Prince of Wales. Shock waves reverberated in London. Henry IV was already feeling somewhat insecure at the time, and he hastened to Wales in an attempt to keep the Welsh 'rebels' in check.

For a while he appeared to succeed, but then he foolishly forced fiercely anti-Welsh legislation through Parliament. From various parts of the country, incensed Welshmen rallied to Owain's cause, and on Good Friday in 1401 hostility erupted. Conwy castle fell to the English in the north, where Henry could use his navy to great effect. So Owain headed south and finally confronted Henry's army where his ships were of little use—on the slopes of Hyddgen in the shadow of Pumlumon. Owain knew the terrain well, and taking full advantage of the peat bogs, won a memorable victory, slaughtering many of Henry's finest men.

Indeed, Owain Glyndwr was to be a thorn in Henry's side for the next eight years. Small wonder the Tudor king attributed magical powers to this Welsh prince, against whom Shakespeare has Henry cry, 'That great magician, damned Glendower!'

As I approached the ruined farm beside Afon Hyddgen (GR780909), heavy clouds were gathering overhead. I sought the refuge of the only serviceable building—a shearing-shed—just as the heavens opened. Hailstones the size of marbles hammered on the corrugated roof. Poor Mike was still somewhere on the open hillside! He later told me that he had crouched in the long grass, with his rucksack covering his head, waiting for the bombardment to cease.

I took advantage of the timely provision of shelter to have some lunch. Quite apart from the sudden downpour, there was a melancholy air about the place. The farm was once home to a couple who reared sheep on these slopes. One winter's night a fierce snowstorm overtook the husband as he checked his flock above Creigiau Bwlch Hyddgen. When he failed to return, his wife, fearing for his safety, lit a lantern and set off to look for him. Both of them perished in the blizzard that night, and the farm soon became derelict. It is said that neighbours marked the place where their bodies were later found huddled together with a circle of white quartz, but I failed to find any evidence of this sad memorial. Even though it was early summer, both the suddenness and the violence of the hail served as a reminder of just how harsh the weather can be in such a high and exposed place.

The heavy shower ended as quickly as it had begun, and I resumed my journey. Crossing the bridge, I followed a track southward that ran parallel to the river. Soon the sun was shining brightly, and I sat for a while on the grassy bank leaning on my rucksack, enjoying the sun's warmth. I must have dozed, for a drop of rain heralding the next shower landed on my face.

On opening my eyes, it was not the darkening sky that caught my attention, however. Soaring in a circle of graceful flight barely fifteen yards away was a red kite. I lay there enthralled, not daring to move. I had known that I was now in kite country, but to see such a majestic bird as close as this, and seemingly quite unconcerned by my presence, was almost unbelievable. I recalled the words I had read earlier in the day:

God, the Maker of heaven and earth, the sea, and everything in them . . . remains faithful for ever.

(Psalm 146:6)

By the time that the kite had disappeared behind Carn Hyddgen, it was raining quite heavily. I was glad it was only rain and not hail, however, and continued walking. Stepping across a tiny trickle of water that flowed across my path down toward the river, I was forced to lengthen my stride to avoid stepping on a brown trout which was wriggling its way across the track. All of seven inches in length, it was far too large to swim freely in such shallow water, but I guess it knew where it was going, for it quickly vanished from sight in one of the numerous channels which drained the hillside.

The rain was still falling steadily as I crossed the narrow bridge spanning Afon Hengwm (GR784892). It was only mid-afternoon, but I had made good progress, having reached almost the halfway point of the traverse. Furthermore, I knew that the narrow cwm leading up to Llyn Llygad Rheidol—the next stage of my journey—was notoriously marshy.

It seemed sensible, therefore, to make use of an ideal spot at which to camp, here on the south side of the river. A well-drained level area of grass, with a low drystone wall as a wind-break and a plentiful supply of water nearby, were all one could ask for. I would be foolish to carry on in the hope of finding anywhere as suitable higher up the valley.

Then Mike arrived and, being of the same mind, pitched his own tent close by, after carrying out a 'first aid' repair to his broken pole. Within half an hour we were joined by a third walker, who was also travelling the 'coast to coast' route. He had actually set out from Llanfairfechan three years earlier, but had been forced to abandon the walk at Machynlleth, suf-fering from heatstroke (not exactly a problem so far, on my journey!). Unable to resume his walk until now, he had returned to Machynlleth that morning, and hoped to reach the Gower in just six days. That meant walking an average of twenty miles a day! He left quite early the following morning, and I never saw him again. I hope he made it in the time he had available—he certainly deserved to.

To camp in such a splendidly isolated place in the company of two other fellow travellers made a welcome change. By now the rain had been replaced by early evening sunshine. We each prepared a hot meal, and then sat talking until the light began to fade. Mike even managed to get a strong enough sig-nal for his mobile phone. I could hear him in his tent talking to his wife. For a while I was just a little envious, but not for long—I was soon asleep.

Distance walked: 8 miles. (Total 85 miles.)

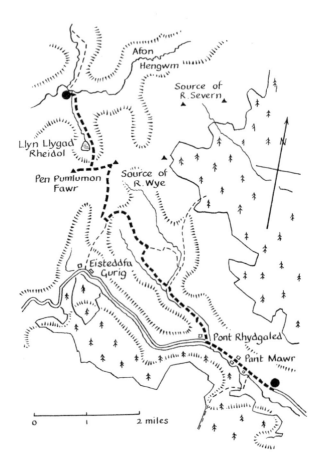

Afon
Hengwm

Source of
R. Severn

Llyn Llygad
Rheidol

Pen Pumlumon
Fawr

Source of
R. Wye

N

Eisteddfa
Gurig

Pont Rhydgaled

Pant Mawr

0   1   2 miles

11
Pumlumon's heights

The new day dawned with the sun shining brightly from a cloudless sky. As I cooked breakfast and packed up, I could anticipate rewarding views from the summit of Pumlumon Fawr with some degree of certainty. I was eager to be on my way.

Mike, with whom I had shared this delightful overnight resting place, was heading north-east to join up with the minor road which links Machynlleth and Staylittle. We therefore bade one another farewell, and I started up Nant-y-llyn. A rather indistinct path follows the stream on its eastern side, and as I climbed, the low-angled sun projected my shadow on to the grassy floor of the valley immediately below. For a moment, I felt strangely detached from reality, watching this silhouette with backpack and trekking-poles mimicking my every move!

The closer I got to Llyn Llygad Rheidol, the more uncertain the course of the path became. Extensive areas of floating moss were now quite common, and increasingly I had to test the ground with each step that I took, to ensure that it would support my weight. The lake was inky-black in colour, even in the bright sunlight. The word *llygad* indicates that this is the source of Afon Rheidol. Standing at this very place nearly one hundred and fifty years before, George Borrow had observed, 'If few rivers have a more wondrous and wild channel than the Rheidol, fewer still have a more beautiful and romantic source.'[1] How truly he spoke! The water was deep, and its surface reflected the steep and craggy amphitheatre that rose up from it. From a distance this forbidding headwall had appeared far too steep to climb in safety. The guidebook, however, spoke of grassy ramps or corridors that led up to the col between Pumlumon Fawr and Pumlumon Fach, and when viewed from the lake, there were clearly several to choose from. Once committed, even to a line that looked fairly straightforward, the route to the top was not always too easy to determine, even as Borrow himself had found when he descended by this route with his guide. As I climbed, I thought of those who might find themselves on such steep and slippery ground descending the mountain in poor visibility. To lose one's footing here could mean a fall of over three hundred feet.

I soon reached the broad saddle, and turned right to follow the wire fence up to the summit cairn and trig point. At last I stood on the top of the 2467-feet-high Pen Pumlumon Fawr. By now a layer of medium-to-high cloud had formed, partially obscuring the sun. Neither was it to be a day of sparklingly clear visibility. Cadair Idris could be seen, but Snowdon was concealed by its own covering of cloud, and so too were the mountains of the south. I was still favoured with excellent weather conditions for this crossing, however, and enjoyed my lunch chatting to four members of a university climbing club, who had walked up from their car parked at the Nant-y-moch Reservoir dam.

With shower clouds now beginning to bubble up in the west, it was time to head east, retracing my steps down to the saddle and on to a rounded plateau where the River Wye has its source (GR800870). From this point another fence follows the spur southwards past the conspicuous cairn on Pen Lluest-y-carn down to where an unsurfaced mountain road, visible below and to the left, contours around a cwm drained by Afon

Cyff (GR802857). There are alternative routes off this range of hills, details of which are found in John Gillham's guidebook. The route I took is not one I can recommend to others, since many of the roads marked on the OS map to the west of y Drum (GR828846) have been acquired by a leading motor manufacturer for testing rally cars, and consequently are fenced off and closed to the public. Admittedly, I neither saw nor heard a rally car as, somewhat furtively, I made my way down, but I did have to ford the River Wye in the absence of any bridge. The river may be in its infancy in these upper reaches, but it was still deep enough for me to discourage others from following my example, and would be even more so following heavy rain.

From this point down to where it joins the A44(T), the road is a public right of way, even if no one had bothered to explain this to the dogs that greeted me as I made my way through the yard of Pont Rhydgaled farm. They proved to be much less of a hazard, however, than the traffic I had to contend with as I cautiously made my way along the main road in the direction of Rhayader.

Before I go any further I really need to 'come clean' and confess that on this particular evening I was not looking for a place to camp. Perhaps 'come clean' is not the best choice of phrase. I had, after all, been walking for nearly a week without being able to have a bath! Tonight I was booked in for bed and breakfast (and bath!) at the Plynlimon Guest House, Pant Mawr. John Gillham recommended this establishment in his guide, and I had already sent one of my food parcels to the address to await my arrival. Unfortunately, the guest house is situated much further along the A44 than either the OS map (which puts Pant Mawr at GR849824) or Gillham in his guide suggests. At GR862818 it means walking a mile and a half along this very busy road, or in my case more than twice that distance, as I turned back before I ever reached it the first time, assuming that I must have inadvertently passed it on the way! This was really something I could have done without. Although I endeavoured to keep as close as I possibly could to the crash barriers at the side of the road, irate motorists still hooted and made threatening gestures. One driver even stopped to tell me how dangerous it was to walk along a main road intended for motor vehicles!

Such antagonism, however, was soon eclipsed by the welcome I received from Ray and Margaret, the proprietors, and the warmth of the bath in which I was soon soaking. Today I had covered another ten miles. A total of ninety-five miles in all meant that I was approaching the halfway mark of my journey. In some ways it had been a day in which no single happening stood out from the rest. But it had been satisfying nevertheless. There had been opportunities to exercise skills and overcome obstacles; to recognise potential danger and take the necessary precautions. I had known the exhilaration of reaching the summit of a mountain; enjoyed magnificent scenery, and walked upon high places. There were streams I'd had to wade through, and unpredictable dogs and unfriendly motorists I had done my best to pacify. Through the day there had been periods of boredom when the landscape seemed slow to change and the miles passed even more slowly, but at its close I had known friendship and hospitality, nourishment and an opportunity to rest.

At the end of the day I reflected on God's goodness to me, from the moment I had awoken that morning. But I also saw reflected in these varied experiences the broader and more expansive tapestry of life lived from day to day. The highs and the lows, the pain and the pleasures, the mundaneness together with the unexpected joys which lift the soul, those things that cause us anxiety and others that instil peace—all have their place. And each one of these things can be the means of bring-ing us closer to God and better able to appreciate the mystery and meaning of life, as he would have us know it.

Distance walked: 10 miles. (Total 95 miles.)

---

1   George Borrow, *Wild Wales*, Gomer Press (1995), p. 460.

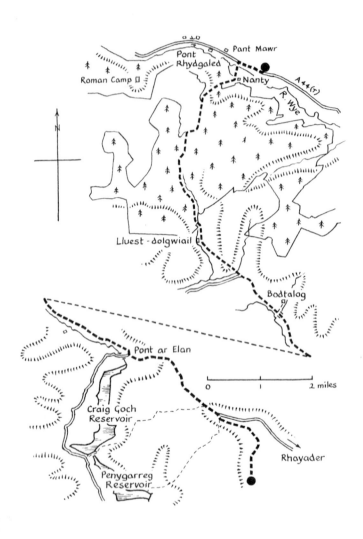

12
Reservoir country

My dream was increasingly being pervaded by the smell of frying bacon. Before opening my eyes I reached out to unzip the entrance of the inner tent in order to prepare a cup of tea. I couldn't find it. The world to which I was slowly waking was one of soft pillows, a warm duvet and a very comfortable mattress. Furthermore, the smell of bacon was not a figment of my dreams—it was for real, wafting up the stairs from the kitchen below and under the bedroom door. It took me no time at all to wash and dress, and I was soon enjoying what was for me the unaccustomed pleasure of a full cooked breakfast, followed by toast and marmalade. Thus fortified, and with no tent to take down or equipment to pack, I was soon ready to say goodbye to my new friends and be on my way. Firstly, I needed to retrace my steps of the previous day to where a path led from the A44 down to a footbridge across the River Wye (GR854820). I even agreed to Ray's kind suggestion that he drive me the half-mile to this location, to avoid antagonising the motorists who were already speeding past the guest house!

As I made my way across the fields towards Nanty, the noise and smell of the traffic was gradually replaced by the fragrance of pine trees carried on a gentle easterly breeze. The sun was shining, and I looked forward to a comparatively easy day, walking fewer miles and with more time for quiet contemplation. Even when walking alone in the mountains, it is frequently possible to be so preoccupied with route finding and the actual logistics of safely negotiating difficult terrain that perhaps little time is available for deeper thought or spiritual reflection. I should make clear at this point that today was Sunday—the day when, as a Christian, I would normally make every effort to meet with others of similar mind and beliefs to worship God and learn more about him. Unfortunately, in spite of much time spent in trying to find a solution to the problem, I had reluctantly come to accept that on this particular Sunday in mid-Wales (a region appropriately described in some guide-books as 'the Great Desert') this would not be possible. I therefore resolved to walk just a few miles, find a quiet place in which to camp, and spend the remainder of the day reading my Bible and enjoying God's company. The fact that things did not turn out as I had either planned or hoped may cause some to question the soundness of such reasoning, or ask why God did not overrule and arrange the day differently. I do not have an answer to that question. What I am sure about is that whilst I was to know frustration, disappointment and fatigue, I never doubted for one minute that God was with me, nor failed to grasp the significance of what he was teaching me that day.

As I climbed up through the forest, firstly west and then south-west from Nanty, the temperature rose. So, too, did the cauliflower cumulus clouds that promised showers later in the day. The road I was following levelled out after a while, and ran along the edge of the forest in a southerly direction, before re-entering the trees and descending to Afon Diliw. I had just been thinking how quiet and restful it was, with birdsong alone breaking the silence, when suddenly the tortuous scream of high-powered chainsaws rent the air. I thought it strange that foresters should be working on a Sunday, when suddenly round the corner roared three leather-clad, masked and helmeted individuals riding massive chainsaws! At least, I thought that's what they were. It was hard to tell when they were generating so much dust and foul-smelling smoke. Ah well! Thankfully peace and quietness were soon restored, even though I was to encounter many more of these characters later in the day.

Emerging from the forest, the path again crossed Afon Diliw and followed the stream south to Lluest Dolgwiail (GR843769). Once more the only building to have survived abandonment and decay was the shearing-shed, and for the second time in three days a threatening sky prompted me to rest awhile under cover and have something to eat. Much later in the day there would be moments when I blamed myself for not stopping here and finding a place to camp for the night. It would certainly have been possible, and had I known then of the restrictions prohibiting all camping that I would encounter later on, I probably would have done so. It was, however, only eleven-thirty in the morning and I had walked but four miles. The thought of stopping so soon just did not occur to me. Instead, I pressed on, diagonally across the south-western flank of Craig y Lluest, and down to join the Cwmystwyth to Rhayader mountain road at GR855758. The view westward down the Ystwyth valley from the crag-bound southern spur of Craig y Lluest should have been worth seeing. In fine weather, this is a place at which to linger. In the event, low cloud now brooding over the moorland had trapped mist in the valley, limiting visibility to just a couple of miles. Having reached a tarmac road, therefore, where I changed into lighter footwear, I determined to press on.

This was now reservoir country, and I had walked less than two miles when I was confronted by the first of many such notices forbidding swimming, fishing, the lighting of fires— and camping. Even now I saw no reason to be too concerned. I had never contemplated putting up my tent by the roadside, and was confident that a friendly farmer would allow me the use of a secluded corner of one of his fields. I was soon to learn, however, that although farmers were indeed friendly, they were subject to the same restrictions and not permitted to allow camping on the land leased to them—a ruling that was apparently enforced by patrolling rangers.

By now I was becoming somewhat frustrated and not a little bemused. Two widely recognised long-distance walks were routed through this remote and beautiful part of mid-Wales, yet no provision seemed to be made for those needing bed and breakfast or youth hostel accommodation or a place to camp. Furthermore, I was still some way from seeing my first reservoir, when I was being told that the reason behind these 'necessary' prohibitions was to prevent polluted water from draining into the lakes. Why then, I wondered, were an increasing number of 4 x 4 vehicles obviously fitted out for rallying, not to mention scores of off-road motorcyclists, many of them sinking up to their axles in a quagmire of their own making, apparently allowed free access to huge areas of surrounding countryside? The damage they were doing to the environment was excessive, whilst the water in several of the streams was obviously contaminated with oil that could only have come from such activity.

By now it was not the absence of somewhere to camp that was my greatest concern. Rather, it was the thoughtless and irresponsible way in which so many, in the name of sport or recreation, were spoiling great swathes of natural moorland, by their noise, exhaust fumes and the sheer amount of physical damage they were inflicting upon a fragile ecosystem. I had begun the day by reading in Psalm 118:24, 'This is the day the LORD has made; let us rejoice and be glad in it.' But faced with such disregard for that which God had created, I felt great heaviness of heart.

Neither did the sight of Craig Goch reservoir from Pont ar Elan, nor the vast dam of Caban-coch reservoir I would visit the following day, do anything to lift my spirit. To me, these great expanses of water lacked the natural beauty of Llyn Idwal, Llynnau Mymbyr or Llyn Gwynant. They were so obviously man-made, and at what terrible expense! The Welsh poet, R. S. Thomas, wrote:[1]

> There are places in Wales I don't go:
> Reservoirs that are the subconscious
> Of a people, troubled far down
> With gravestones, chapels, villages even.

And I believe I know what he felt. How many of the hundreds of visitors that now picnic on their banks, or marvel at the mighty achievements of civil engineers a hundred years ago, pause to consider the heartbreak and sense of upheaval felt by those whose homes and community now lie drowned under 11,000 million gallons of water? Of course, I appreciate that the people of Birmingham need water, just as we all benefit from electricity even when it may have been generated by nuclear power. Furthermore, as a lay person I do not pretend to know where alternative sources of water or energy may be found. But that does not stop me being saddened or concerned about those things that, in the name of 'progress', drastically change or possibly endanger a long-established order or way of life.

Perhaps, as a Christian, I am also looking beyond the physical flooding of a valley and the material loss of farms and villages, seeing embodied in these 'achievements' the far more serious consequences of a whole nation that has been inundated by secularism, and obsessed with wealth, success and power. There have certainly been, in the history of our land, times when, in spite of poverty and poor health (some might even say, *because of* such things), people acknowledged God and sought to live according to the teaching of his Word, the Bible. Faith, truth and righteousness before God were spiritual values that mattered, and that formed the bedrock of a stable society. Now, alas, such things have been swept aside. In a 'scientific' age it is no longer fashionable to believe in God or to take seriously the claims of Christ. Heaven and hell are no longer relevant. They lie buried beneath the murky depths of a philosophy that puts man at its centre, and has human achievement and personal happiness as its ultimate goal. How sad!

The reader may rightly surmise that I was not sorry to head both eastwards and upwards away from Pont ar Elan, and for today at least turn my back on these rather characterless stretches of water. The Rhayader road climbed steeply for a mile to reach a height of 1600 feet. By now I was becoming quite tired and was anxious to find somewhere to spend the night. There was a commercial campsite marked on the map at Rhayader, but that would take me well off my planned route and add to tomorrow's mileage. In any case, it was still almost four miles away by road, and my feet were already suffering from the distance I had walked that day on tarmac. With a food parcel to be collected tomorrow in Elan Village, I therefore decided to leave the mountain road and head south along the foot of Craig Ddu and Cefn Rhydoldog. There were several farms in this area, and I felt sure that one of them would have somewhere for me to spend the night. It was good to be walking on rough paths once again, even if the sky was growing ominously dark. I kept looking at my watch, finding it hard to believe that it was only five o'clock. Heavy drops of rain began to fall as I approached the first farm. Dogs barked noisily to announce my arrival—at least fifty of them, in actual fact, for I appeared to have stumbled upon the local hunt kennels. I was almost relieved to find nobody at home, and have an excuse to go on a little further.

I would hesitate to describe the next residence as a 'farm'. A magnificent house surrounded by beautiful gardens was set against the backdrop of a tree-covered hillside. Although I was walking on a public right of way, I approached with awe, feeling that I had no business to be there. Indeed, my initial reaction was to continue even further, rather than trouble those that lived there, when I saw a kindly looking gentleman beside a silver-coloured Mercedes—cleaning a mountain bike! Greatly encouraged by the sight, I approached. The man in question was a retired Ghurka Regiment army officer who had just returned from trekking in Nepal. Telling me that he knew exactly what it was like to search for a suitable place to camp at the end of a long day, he led me to what he described as the 'tennis court'—a level area of sheep-cropped grass at the edge of a field facing down the valley toward Rhayader. I guess you don't embrace retired army officers, but I did the next best thing and shook his hand warmly. I would later discover that the owners of the estate were associated with one of the best-known producers of printed textiles in Wales.

The rain clouds had by now dispersed and the evening sun was shining. Yes, I was tired, and the day had certainly not turned out as I had planned. In fact I had walked sixteen miles, nearly half of them on a hard road-surface. But as I sat in the entrance of my tent preparing a most welcome meal, I was at peace. Sheep grazed contentedly all around me, while overhead three red kites soared in graceful circles. What if my legs did ache a little, and my feet were rather sore? At the end of the day God had provided me with the choicest of places in which to rest, and I could now spend the remaining hours in fellowship with him.

Distance walked: 16 miles. (Total 111 miles.)

---

1   R. S. Thomas, *Selected Poems, 1946–68*, Bloodaxe Books Ltd. (1986), p. 105.

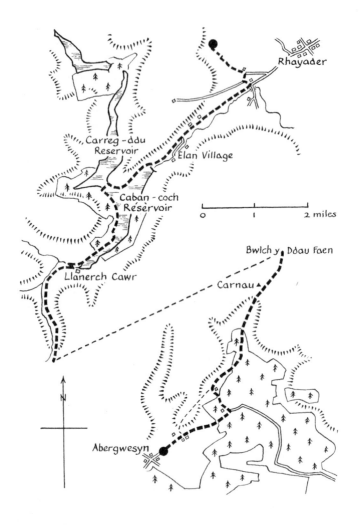

13
From Elan to
Abergwesyn

Day dawned bright and fair. After a good night's rest, any soreness from the previous evening seemed to have gone, and I prepared to move off. Again I thanked the genial owner on whose land I had been allowed to camp, and we waved farewell to each other as I set off down the lane. In fifteen minutes I had reached the road which ran south-west from Rhayader and followed it beside the river to Elan Village.

Enjoying an early morning cup of coffee in the hotel, I learnt from the receptionist of the concern caused by the arrival, by post, of my food parcel. Before posting any of these two-kilogram packages, I naturally telephoned those to whom they would be sent, to make sure they were happy with such an arrangement. Unfortunately, the person to whom I spoke at this particular 'staging post', and who told me they would be perfectly willing to help in this way, then left for a short break without telling anyone else on the staff of what she had done.

At any other time this would hardly have mattered. The problem arose only because, at the same time that the parcel arrived addressed to myself and marked 'To await collection', the hotel was being alerted to the possibility of dangerous packages being sent through the post! Nobody on the staff seemed to know who this mysterious 'M. Perrin' might be or what the parcel could possibly contain. I am not too sure where the suspect package was deposited, but there seemed to have been a certain amount of understandable anxiety until the member of staff returned from her break and allayed their fears. I was also somewhat relieved that my pasta, dried fruit and powdered milk had not been scattered across the countryside in a controlled explosion carried out by the bomb squad from Hereford!

Very soon, the massive sweep of stone and concrete of the Caban-coch dam came into view. This is the last and therefore lowest of the four dams, retaining almost five hundred acres of water, whilst allowing nearly 30,000 gallons a day to flow into the River Wye by way of compensation. It is said that a fox once scrambled halfway up the face of the dam, to escape pursuing hounds.

There is a very well-laid-out Visitor Centre just beneath the dam, with a restaurant, an exhibition, and a gift-shop selling postcards and tea towels bearing pictures of red kites. Upon entering, I was handed a questionnaire and invited to give my impressions of the Trust's administration of the reservoir area. I mischievously asked for three or four extra sheets of paper, and may well have given unintentional offence when asked to explain myself! They clearly were not accustomed to visitors expressing anything other than great pleasure and appreciation. My comments relating to the activities of off-road vehicles were received with some sympathy. They told me they recognised the problem, but added that to allow camping of any description would be quite contrary to Trust policy and would open the way to large-scale misuse of the environment. I continued on my way none the wiser, and with no advice to offer fellow walkers, save this: Prepare for a long day, and make for Rhayader!

My route now lay along the northern shore of Caban-coch reservoir, across the stone bridge and down to its southernmost tip. The western margin was not unattractive. The wooded slopes leading down to the water's edge were covered with bluebells, although by this time the sun had disappeared and a rising northerly wind was beginning to chill the air.

They were gathering the sheep at Llannerch Cawr farm— a major undertaking involving a number of helpers from neighbouring farms. A team of specialist builders were also at work, giving to such a remote location an air of busy activity this particular morning. Several of the older farms in this area were examples of the ancient longhouse pattern, where the family would live at one end, with the animals housed at the other. One such dwelling, which would have been destroyed with the construction of the Claerwen dam, was dismantled and rebuilt at the National Folk Museum situated at St. Fagan's, near Cardiff. Llannerch Cawr is another example, and was currently undergoing extensive preservation work. I talked for a while with the owner, and also enjoyed a tele-phone conversation with my wife, before setting off up a farm road which climbed into the hills above Afon Rhiwnant.

The mountain crossing to Abergwesyn would be six miles by the most direct route, climbing to 1762 feet at Carnau (GR889578); but having had a long and tiring walk the previous day, I was quite prepared, and indeed had sought permission at the farm, to camp midway. Had the weather been more favourable, I would undoubtedly have done this, for the scenery was most attractive. As I gained height, however, the wind increased to almost gale force. The showers that were now being swept in from the north and falling as rain in the valleys took the form of driving sleet higher up. I was glad to be heading south, and therefore facing away from such an unseasonable onslaught, but it was hard to believe that this was early summer rather than February or March. Hardly surprisingly, the idea of camping high on the hills lost some of its appeal, and being blown along by the wind I was carried on up and over Carnau in the hope of finding shelter in the lee of the mountain.

There were few signs of any track leading from Carnau down to the forest. Nant Gerwynhad carved a deep gully in the shaly rock, whilst away from this ravine the hillside was covered with clumps of rushes, making for difficult walking. At GR883565 there was access to the forest, however, and a path through the trees led down to where it was possible to ford the stream flowing from Nant Melyn. A forest road climbed southwards from the stream, but upon reaching an area where widespread felling had taken place, I left the road on a rough track heading south-west and out of the forest. Sheltered from the wind and enjoying some improvement in the weather, pleasant walking across the fields led towards a farm nestling below a small tree-filled defile that cut into the hillside. This having all the appearance of a holiday home rather than a working farm, and with nobody answering my knock on the door, I really should have continued on the same path to the north of Bryn Clun and descended to Glangwesyn. Instead, I chose to follow the track to Trallwm (yet more holiday homes), and from there, by way of the lane from Beulah, down to Abergwesyn.

By the time I had reached the site of the former phone box—the one marked on the OS map at GR863533 has now been moved a quarter of a mile further down the road—I realised that the upper part of this delightful valley was almost exclusively 'holiday home' country. Locked doors, shuttered windows, overgrown gardens and empty driveways were very much the order of the day. I will forbear entering into a debate on this vexed subject, which has generated so much resentment and hostility in the past. My only comment on the issue would be this. I am always saddened when I find a cottage or farmstead which was once home to a growing family—or, worse still, a village which was at one time a thriving community—now standing empty and silent for nine months of the year. I could so easily have erected my tent and spent the night on land attached to any one of these properties, and no one would have been any the wiser. But how much more would I have preferred to spend time talking with a local farmer, and being permitted to sleep in the shelter of a stone wall which daily witnessed the hardships and rewards of a working hill farm!

I had particularly wanted to come to Abergwesyn because of its association with one of Wales's great men of God. Later in my walk I would have the thrill of visiting Pantycelyn, home to one of our most famous hymn-writers, William Williams (1717–91).

Williams was born at Cefn-coed near Llandovery. His parents wished him to study medicine and sent him to a college near Hay. Hay was but seven miles from Talgarth, a town at the centre of the ministry of Howell Harris, another great preacher and a founder of Welsh Methodism. Indeed, it was in the churchyard at Talgarth that the twenty-year-old student of medicine first heard Harris preach. The truth of the Christian message penetrated his heart, and the power of God firstly convicted him of his sinfulness and then, within days, led him to know full and free forgiveness through faith in Christ.

It was not long before Williams was persuaded that God wanted him to be a physician of men's souls, and he was encouraged by Harris and Daniel Rowland of Llangeitho to seek ordination to the Anglican ministry. Three years later, in 1740, he was ordained by the Bishop of St David's and appointed as a curate to serve in Abergwesyn. In such a sparsely populated area, he soon longed to reach far more than those who simply resided in the parish. (We may wonder how he would have felt today, with so many dwellings now holiday homes and empty for much of .the year!) As a result, he began to follow the example of Howell Harris, and took to travelling around the surrounding district, preaching wherever there were people who would listen. His parishioners strongly disapproved of this practice and complained to the bishop, with the result that Williams's one and only brief curacy came to an end. In 1964 the parish church in the village was pulled down, but the close, if brief, connection between Abergwesyn and one of my great 'heroes' made my being here very special indeed.

Still in need of somewhere to spend the night, I was leaning on the bridge, wondering whether anyone would object to my camping by Afon Gwesyn, when a vehicle pulled into a house nearby. One dwelling, at least, was occupied, and it was not very long before I had made the acquaintance of Dudley and his wife. They showed me great kindness, making me a cup of tea, letting me use their telephone, and even offering me the use of a holiday cottage for which they had responsibility. I was most grateful, but preferred to camp if at all possible.

It was Sue and Eifion, living with their three sons just two hundred yards down the road, who came to my assistance. Eifion farmed locally, while his wife was a district nurse. They, too, were most generous in their hospitality, and offered me the floor of their son's playroom on which to sleep that night, for by now it was raining again and the wind was rising. But they also had well-drained and sheltered land below their house, and I was able to convince them that I was well able to spend a comfortable night in the open and get enough rest to continue with my journey the next day.

116

I was deeply touched by the kindness shown by all these folk to one who was a stranger, and left the following morning after having joined the family for breakfast, feeling that in a comparatively short time real friendships had been forged.

Distance walked: 14 miles. (Total 125 miles.)

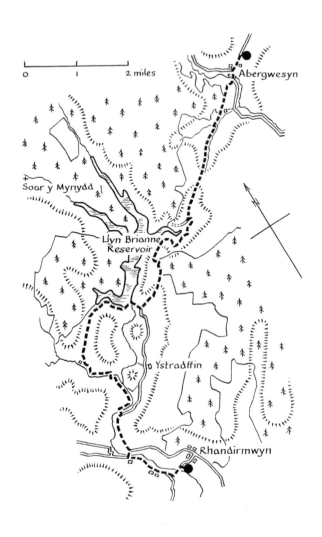

Abergwesyn

0   1   2 miles

Soar y Mynydd

Llyn Brianne
Reservoir

Ystradffin

Rhandirmwyn

14
Llyn Brianne

It was overcast but dry when I left the farm and set off down the lane. My first stop was to be the churchyard in the village. There is something particularly poignant about the wording on the map: *Church (rems. of)*. As one who has always believed that a church is comprised of people rather than stone, bricks and mortar, perhaps I ought not to feel too emotional if a mere building, for whatever reason, no longer exists. But I cannot help but equate, in my mind, an ancient meeting place dedicated to the service of God with the spiritual life of the community round about. When one goes, surely the other must suffer.

Arriving at the iron gateway, I soon discovered that even the words *'rems. of'* were something of an exaggeration. *'Site of'* would be nearer the mark, for of 'remains' none existed that I could find. Just a gathering of gravestones in a sea of cow-parsley, and an ancient moss-crowned Celtic cross standing like a sentinel among the yew trees. William Williams appears to have been right. When the Christian gospel is confined within four walls, it does not take root—it withers and dies.

A hundred yards beyond the churchyard and on the far side of Afon Irfon, a forestry road winds up the hillside. At the point at which it entered the forest, I turned off to the left on a track that led south-west to a large building that was once a hotel. A third of a mile further on, just beyond the confluence of two streams, the path divides. The right-hand fork ascends the ridge back into the Tywi Forest, while the other follows the stream in a south-westerly direction toward the eastern arm of the Llyn Brianne reservoir. Taking the second of these, progress to the *bwlch* (GR828504) was both wearying and wet. Any semblance of a path was soon lost amongst the bracken and dense clumps of sallow. Frequent showers from the north-east swept up the valley, whilst the wet vegetation and boggy ground underfoot all contributed to a general feeling of dampness. A much firmer path dropped down to the road below Esgair Garn, and in the lee of the hills the weather improved slightly.

I found Llyn Brianne more visually attractive than the reservoirs of the Elan Valley. From its four distinct 'arms', the hillsides rise steeply from the water's edge. Though largely forested, the irregular planting of a mixture of both conifers and deciduous trees made a welcome change from the more familiar rectangular 'blocks' of fir trees that so often disfigure the landscape. The southern slopes provided rough grazing for a large herd of mountain ponies, whilst other areas had been given over to bracken and gorse, much to the delight of the many whinchat that greeted my arrival with their metallic 'tic-tic' alarm call, and brief but pleasant warbling song.

I sat by the road looking up the north-westerly arm of the reservoir. Poor visibility and a folding of the hills hid Soar-y-mynydd from view, but I recalled just how much that remote Welsh valley meant to the late Dr D. Martyn Lloyd-Jones. On the OS map, a chapel is the only building indicated (GR785533), but it meant everything to those whose farms were scattered among the surrounding hills. Dr Lloyd-Jones is best remembered for his powerful preaching to large congregations in Westminster Chapel from 1938 to 1968, and I count myself privileged indeed to have benefited personally under that ministry during my days as a student in London. But I would dare to suggest that the 'Doctor' was never happier or more eloquent than when preaching, as he regularly did in the 1930s, to the congregation that gathered at Soar-y-mynydd. His beloved wife Bethan describes the scene on one occasion:

> I remember this Sunday best because it was a glorious day, and the beauty of the scenery indescribable. I shall never forget the sight, looking down at the chapel in the valley, while still some four miles away. Half a dozen or more paths led down to it from various directions, and these were all alive with streams of ponies (bearing the congregation!) converging on the little grey-stone jewel in its lush green setting.
>
> On arrival, the great stable under the church was soon full to its doors, and the rest of the ponies were turned out to the near-by field or enclosure. Then we all trooped into the little chapel and soon filled it. Every farmer had his devoted sheep dog sitting between his feet, behaving perfectly and seemingly enjoying everything to the full. We never had trouble with the dogs, though occasionally there was the sound of a short, sharp fracas from beneath, as the ponies in the stable below had an argument. This morning we counted over seventy ponies. As for the service, never in the whole of Wales would one find a more attentive and appreciative congregation, and the singing was joyous.[1]

My route took me north off the mountain road and across the dam. One or two cars had pulled into the car park, but their occupants saw no reason to get out. A cold wind blew across the water, and the air was damp with drizzle. It was lunchtime, so I sat below the parapet and soon had a packet of thick farmhouse vegetable soup simmering on the stove. To prepare hot food at midday was certainly not my normal practice, but somehow conditions on this occasion seemed to warrant it. Then it was on to the most westerly tip of Llyn Brianne before heading south-west to Troed-rhiw-ruddwên. Once again, by descending into a valley sheltered from the wind, there was a distinct improvement in the weather.

A narrow lane led from the farm alongside Afon Doethie, and before long I was sitting on a rocky outcrop high above this river's wild confluence with the Tywi. Somewhere, high among the oak trees that clothed the conical hill called Dinas, was the cave of Twm Shon Cati. Whether he ever lived among the rocks in this magnificent place is doubtful. Indeed, so many stories have been told about this colourful character that it is virtually impossible to separate truth from legend. Born Thomas Jones, about 1530, near Tregaron, he was a man of some means, a bard, and an expert in heraldry. He was also something of an adventurer, whose exploits as a Welsh 'Robin Hood' were recorded in a book by Thomas Pritchard, published in 1828 and entitled *The Adventures and Vagaries of Twm Shon Catti*. His second wife, whom he married in 1607, came from Ystrad-ffin on the far side of Dinas.

The road now continued south along the beautiful upper reaches of the Tywi valley. I stopped briefly to chat to a couple who were experiencing their very first backpacking 'holiday'. He told me that he was carrying a pack weighing 80 pounds! I had no way of verifying this, but from the size of the tent strapped beneath his rucksack he could well have been correct. I felt some sympathy for the man when he learnt that my own sack, weighing less than 35 pounds, contained all that I required for a three-week journey. It may have been their first holiday spent in this way. As I left them, I found myself hoping it would not be their last.

From the bridge across the Tywi (GR773460), it is possible to follow a path along the west side of the river, or alternatively take the more direct route along the road which comes from Llyn Brianne. Either way leads to the whitewashed and welcoming Tywi Bridge Inn. Elaine and I had camped here in

1983 when we were cycling in the area, and well remember the peacocks that belonged to the owner. They were not only very colourful, but were also among the most inquisitive creatures I have ever met, for we seemed to spend most of our time discouraging them from either entering the tent or emptying the contents of our panniers. I looked for them again in vain. No raucous call broke the silence; no vivid display of colour was anywhere to be seen. Perhaps, sadly I thought, they may have ransacked just one tent too many!

Keeping to the south-west bank of the river, I walked on to Rhandir-mwyn. Crossing back over the Tywi brought me to a very smart and well-equipped campsite. There are several sites in the valley, but this was the only one whose address I had been able to obtain and to which I could therefore send a parcel. After camping in the wild or on farmland, I felt quite out of place among the expensive camper vans and almost house-sized frame tents! But the showers and laundry facilities were more than a luxury—by now they were a dire necessity, and I took full advantage of both. I also much enjoyed a meal of mince with mashed potatoes followed by peaches and custard, while one after another of my fellow 'campers' approached to enquire both how and why anyone of my more 'mature' years could possibly sleep in a tent so small, or survive for so long with as little 'luggage'!

As I settled down for a very comfortable night's sleep, listening to someone in the distance trying to start their Mercedes camper, I was smugly satisfied in the knowledge that the less you have, the less there is to lose or go wrong.

Distance walked: 12 miles. (Total 137 miles.)

1   Iain H. Murray, *D. Martyn Lloyd-Jones, the First Forty Years 1899–1939*, The Banner of Truth Trust (1982), p. 322.

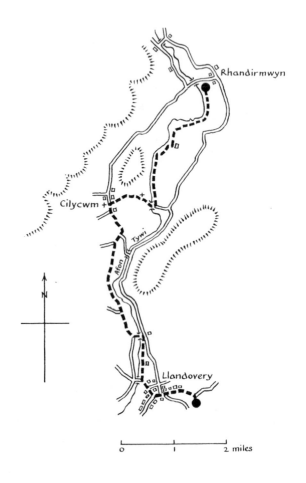

Rhandirmwyn

Cilycwm +

Afon Tywi

N

Llandovery

0   1   2 miles

15
Sunshine and shadow

What a glorious way to begin a day's walking! To wake up to bright sunshine, pack away a dry tent, and then simply climb over a stile in a corner of the campsite to find yourself on a delightful path that wanders among the trees on the bank of the beautiful River Tywi.

To begin with, it was a level path keeping close company with a slow-moving, tranquil stretch of water; then, a track climbing steeply among the trees to avoid a rocky gorge through which the river tumbled and rushed with a sense of urgency. Emerging from the woods, my path crossed two fields to a small cottage (GR772423), where it joined a narrow lane running south. For some time now, hedges had replaced the familiar drystone walls in the north of the country, but these that now bordered my lane were 'proper' hedges. Not manicured privet or box, but a dense mixture of hazel and blackthorn, in the shade of which grew fern and foxglove, and whose branches were intertwined with honeysuckle and traveller's joy—a veritable wildlife 'sanctuary' which had taken centuries to develop and hopefully would remain for as long.

I paused in a gateway that led into a field. Only twenty yards away, a red kite was stripping the last remnants from the carcass of a rabbit, before rising majestically into the air. These wonderful birds feed mainly on carrion, and since it has been recognised that they pose little threat to farm stock, their increase both in numbers and distribution has become one of the great 'success stories' of conservation of the last thirty years.

Arriving at a T-junction, I turned right to cross the river on my way to Cil-y-cwm. Standing on the bridge and looking down into the dark, still water of the Tywi, I was at once overcome by a feeling of melancholy as I thought just how much Carl would have loved the sights and sounds that had given me such pleasure already that morning. Carl was the second of our three sons. His last few years had been happily spent in Ethiopia, where he had worked as a water engineer with Tear Fund,[1] but he was tragically drowned in the swollen floodwaters of a tributary of this very river—Afon Cothi, which flows into the Tywi between Llandeilo and Carmarthen. He died in 1992 at the age of twenty-eight. He would have been thirty-five now. How dearly I would have loved to share some of this journey with him! As Christians, my wife and I have the deep assurance that he is with Christ and that one day we shall see him again—a God-given hope which saw us through those dark days immediately following his death. But we are also human beings, and were anyone to tell me that the pain gets less as the years pass, I would have to disagree with them. Of course, life must go on for those that remain, and the comfort derived from our faith in God's unerring providence is precious indeed. But there are still times when we miss Carl so very much; occasions when memories come flooding back and the tears return. And standing on the bridge over the Tywi this morning was one such occasion. I am not ashamed of this, nor do I imagine that God holds this against me or chastens me for surrendering to earthly grief. He who knew what it was to see his own Son suffer and die on a cross for the sins of his people, knew exactly what I was feeling and once again comforted me as no one else could.

Little more that a quarter of a mile from the bridge, a Calvinistic Methodist chapel stood at the side of the lane. Its pale yellow painted walls gave it a bright and 'well-kept' appearance. Swallows were swooping to and from their nests under the eaves, while a sundial built into the front wall told me it was ten-thirty. An hour slow, I thought to myself, as I looked at my watch, but then British Summer Time would have meant nothing to the men who placed it here in 1740 when the chapel was built. There was no one around to ask about its history, nor whether it was still used today and by how many. But two hundred and sixty years is a long time, and this area had known much blessing from God's hand during that period. What great preaching had been listened to and how many lives had been touched within the walls of this sanctuary, I wondered? And, more to the point —was God still at work here, in our own troubled times?

It was one man in particular that made me want to visit Cil-y-cwm. I have for several years loved a hymn which runs:

> When oceans vast their depths reveal
>   And moons have ceased to wane,
> The Lamb who died and rose again,
>   On Zion's hill shall reign.
>
> His glorious Name must long endure
>   When suns have ceased to shine,
> And through eternity, the saints
>   Will sing His praise divine.
>
> As countless as the drops of dew,
>   Or sand upon the shore,
> Are blessings which the ransomed have
>   In Him for evermore.
>
> Let every other name recede,
>   His Name alone extol;
> In Him reserved, there is the grace
>   To satisfy my soul.

The author was a man named Morgan Rhys of Cil-y-cwm (1716–79). He is not particularly well known to English congregations, for few of his hymns were ever translated. He wrote prolifically in Welsh, however, and published several

127

collections of hymns, many of which are widely known and sung today. He joined the Calvinistic Methodists and, in 1757, became a teacher in one of the 'circulating schools'. So called because they moved from place to place, these classes were started by Griffith Jones of Llanddowror to teach the poor to read the Bible and instruct them in the great truths of the Christian faith. Morgan Rhys died in 1779 and was buried at Llanfynydd, where incidentally our own son Carl was also laid to rest.

I had hoped to find out a little more about Rhys by visiting the parish church with its solidly built square stone tower. There were booklets to take away and displays to study giving much information about the architecture; but regarding any local men who may have been used by God, or times of great blessing that might have occurred, I could find absolutely nothing. Walking down a side road opposite, I came to Capel-y-groes, another Methodist chapel whose stonework had been painted—this time an attractive shade of pink. There was no mention of him here either. The date above the entrance was 1859, some eighty years after Morgan Rhys had died. This, however, was the year that one of the greatest revivals had swept across Wales, so clearly this little village had known something of God's power and blessing at that time also. Indeed, contemporary records state that about two hundred people from this relatively small community were affected and added to this one church alone that year, as were many in the village of Rhandir-mwyn. One historian wrote at the time concerning this neighbourhood, 'It may be said that nothing is now left to the devil but a few gleanings; the large sheaves are in the possession of the Lord of the harvest.'[2]

Unable to find out anything more about Morgan Rhys, and it being lunchtime, I went into the Newydd Fawr Arms for a ploughman's lunch. I was grappling with the rather strange name, which to me seemed to translate into the 'Big New

Arms', when a group of five local farmers entered. They greeted me warmly and wanted to know where I had come from and in which direction I was heading. They then sat at the next table and proceeded to discuss the latest livestock prices—in English. Now I know that there are those who fear that by speaking Welsh in the presence of an English person they may possibly give offence, and who try to avoid doing so by choosing to converse in English. I have never understood why, and have always felt uncomfortable whenever folk have done this. I therefore smiled appreciatively, but then told them, in Welsh, to feel free to speak their mother tongue. I really don't know who was more embarrassed, they or I, when they replied that apart from Fred, who knew just a few odd words, not one of them could speak Welsh! This probably went some way to explaining the strange name that had been given to the inn.

Rested and well-nourished, I continued on my way. The sun was still shining brightly as I took the road on the western side of the river, this seeming to be the quieter of the two roads, both of which led south to Llandovery. A mile north of the town I crossed the Tywi, however, to take advantage of a footpath that appeared to follow the river all the way into the town. It is, in fact, now necessary to make a small detour away from the river and around a farm at GR763353, but this is still preferable to walking along either of the two roads.

As a small market town, I suspect Llandovery has changed little since George Borrow passed through in the November of 1854. Indeed, sensing it to be a place in which very little of significance occurs today, I called to mind two episodes Borrow himself chose to relate. The first concerned Twm Shon Cati who, in his more roguish days, entered an ironmonger's shop in the town under the pretext of wanting to purchase an iron porridge pot. When the poor shopkeeper had produced three or four of his best pots for inspection, Tom complained that one had a hole in it. As he peered into its dark interior declaring that he could see no such hole, Tom forcibly rammed the pot over the unfortunate man's head, exclaiming 'There *is* a hole in the pot, otherwise how could you have got your head inside?' By the time the ironmonger had succeeded in removing the offending pot, Tom had gathered up the other pots and run from the shop!

An infinitely more remarkable event described by Borrow was the conversion of Rhys Prichard, who was the vicar of Llandovery some two centuries before the linguist and long-distance walker ever visited the town. Born in Llandovery in 1575 and sent to Oxford at the age of eighteen to study theology, he misspent his student days in wanton behaviour and drunkenness. Indeed, his lifestyle changed little when he returned to Llandovery and was appointed vicar, and he was frequently observed being pushed in a wheelbarrow from the public house to the vicarage after a bout of excessive drinking —a sad example, which dissolute parishioners were quick to exploit. 'Bad as we may be, we are not half so bad as the parson!' was an oft-heard excuse following a night's revelry.

One night Rhys Prichard derived perverse amusement from sharing his ale with a goat that had followed him into the bar. When the besotted animal lay on the floor quivering in a drunken stupor, the vicar roared with delight. The following evening, however, when he had determined to entertain himself in the same fashion, the by now wiser he-goat merely sniffed the beer before turning away in disgust and hurrying from the room. Such surprising behaviour from so lowly a creature struck Rhys Prichard's heart and conscience. 'How different is its conduct to mine!' he is reported to have exclaimed:

I, after having experienced a hundred times the filthiness and misery of drunkenness, have still persisted in debasing myself below the condition of a beast. O, if I persist in this conduct, what have I to expect but wretchedness and contempt in this world, and eternal perdition in the next? But, thank God, it is not yet too late to amend; I am still alive— I will become a new man—the goat has taught me a lesson.

Smashing his clay pipe and leaving a full glass of ale on the table, he returned to the vicarage a changed man. In George Borrow's own words, 'different as an angel of light is from the fiend of the pit was Rees Pritchard from that moment from what he had been in former days'.[3] For more than thirty years he preached the gospel faithfully and with powerful results. Furthermore, he had a great talent for versification and used it to express moral and spiritual truths, his writings being published after his death under the title of *Canwyll y Cymry* ('The Candle of the Welshmen'). One of the best-known of these, 'God's Better than All', epitomises this new life, and begins:

> God's better than heaven or aught therein,
> Than the earth or aught we there can win,
> Better than the world or its wealth to me—
> God's better than all that is or can be.

The campsite where I intended to spend the next two nights lay half a mile out of Llandovery on the A40(T). It was set back from the main road, however, and the facilities were adequate. Furthermore, given my plans for the following day, it was ideally located. As I enjoyed my pasta and date custard, a glorious sunset provided a grand finale to what had been a truly excellent day.

Distance walked: 8 miles. (Total 145 miles.)

---

1   The Evangelical Alliance Relief Fund, a Christian relief agency working in the Third World.
2   Thomas Phillips, op. cit., pp. 24-5.
3   George Borrow, *Wild Wales*, Gomer Press (1995), p. 512.

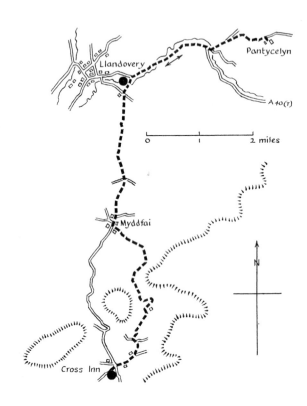

Pantycelyn

Llandovery

A 40(T)

0   1   2 miles

Myddfai

N

Cross Inn

16
Pantycelyn

Leaving most of my equipment at the campsite in order to travel as lightly as possible, I set off along the A40(T) in the direction of Brecon. I have already aired the problems facing the walker who, on occasions, has no alternative but to walk such unpleasant and dangerous sections of trunk road. As with the A44(T), where crash barriers rather than roadside verges are the order of the day, the main road between Llandovery and Brecon is definitely not for the faint-hearted or flat-footed!

Furthermore, I was going to have to walk nearly two miles before being able to turn off on to quieter lanes; and then I would have the very same hazards to face on the return journey. For this was to be a loop or detour of some six miles off my main route. Having said that, I had been looking forward to this morning with all my heart. I was going to Pantycelyn.

I mentioned William Williams (1717–91) in chapter fourteen. His brief ministry as a curate in the Anglican church had taken him to Abergwesyn. It was his much longer ministry in his own home, however, for which he is best remembered. So much so that his name will forever be linked with the name of the house in which he spent his married life, and where he wrote so many of his great hymns—William Williams of Pantycelyn, 'the sweet singer of Wales'.

There surely cannot be a Welshman or woman, nor few English come to that, who will not have sung the words:

Guide me, O Thou great Jehovah,
  Pilgrim through this barren land;
I am weak, but Thou art mighty,
  Hold me with Thy powerful hand;
    Bread of heaven,
  Feed me till I want no more.

Its author was William Williams.[1] On frequent occasions, it has to be said, the most rousing renditions of this great hymn have not come from those who share its writer's spiritual-mindedness or godly manner of life. But for all its misuse, it remains one of the most cherished hymns sung by Christians around the world.

Whilst this has to be the best-known of the 123 hymns that appeared in English, it was the 993 he penned in Welsh that have endeared him to the people of Wales. 'He impressed the stamp of his genius for ever on Welsh literature', someone once wrote. 'While a Welsh heart responds to its God in its own tongue, the hymns of William Williams will live.'[2] And this morning I am to visit his home.

Leaving the traffic of the main road behind, I relaxed and began to enjoy the quiet, leafy lanes that led eastward along a valley protected on either side by green rolling hills. I was somewhat surprised to see the signposts directing me toward Babel. Until then I had not noticed the name on the map. I was even more perplexed by the sound of repeated explosions in the distance. Who or what could be responsible for these continuous detonations in an otherwise tranquil world? Then I noticed another name on the map: Sennybridge, accompanied by the warning: *Danger Area—Artillery Range*. Perhaps Babel was not such an inappropriate name after all.

Trying to close my mind to this regular noise of bombardment, I concentrated on the hedges festooned with rosebay willowherb, meadowsweet, vetch and heady-scented honeysuckle.

With no one else within earshot, I even tried to drown the sound of gunfire by 'singing'. One my favourite hymns by William Williams seemed especially appropriate:

> Speak, I pray Thee, gentle Jesus!
>   O how passing sweet Thy words,
> Breathing o'er my troubled spirit
>   Peace which never earth affords.
> All the world's distracting voices,
>   All the enticing tones of ill,
> At Thy accents mild, melodious,
>   Are subdued and all is still.
>
> Tell me Thou art mine, O Saviour,
>   Grant me an assurance clear;
> Banish all my dark misgivings,
>   Still my doubting, calm my fear.
> O, my soul within me yearneth
>   Now to hear Thy voice divine;
> So shall grief be gone for ever
>   And despair no more be mine.[3]

Unlike some hymn-writers, who always seem to write in a triumphalist manner of brightness, joy and victory, Williams was a realist who knew that even the most spiritual person can be subject to fear and doubt. I am sure that it is because I have so frequently known such times in my own Christian life that this most moving of hymns remains one of my favourites.

It was mid-morning when I reached the farm. I was not expected and had even prepared myself for the possibility of there being nobody at home. The barking of the dogs quelled that fear, however, and I was soon making the acquaintance of today's Mr Williams. Shortly after the death of William Williams' father John in 1742, his mother Dorothy had inherited Pantycelyn from her brother. William, having resigned his curacy at Abergwesyn in 1744, married Mary Francis in 1749, and here they were to live until his death in 1791. The farm has remained in the Williams family to this day, and whilst there has not been an unbroken line of descent from father to son, the Mr Williams who so kindly welcomed me into the house is a sixth-generation descendant of the hymn-writer. I found the whole experience of being in the sitting room, with the very grandfather clock that stood there in William Williams' day still ticking away the seconds, a very emotional one.

And so had others, judging from the entries in the visitors' book that I was invited to sign. A week or two before, a group of Korean pastors had visited the farm. The very first Protestant missionary to be martyred in Korea in 1866 was a Welshman named Robert Jermain Thomas. Born in Rhayader in 1840, where his father was a Congregational minister, the family later moved to Llanover near Abergavenny. Converted to Christ as a teenager, Robert's gifts and calling were later recognised by his home church and, after studying in London for six years, he left for China under the auspices of the London Missionary Society in 1863.

It was not long before the spiritual needs of Korea were laid upon his heart by God, and after studying the language he determined to preach the gospel in that land. Travelling by riverboat, both his preaching and the Bibles he distributed were well received until, upon the orders of the king, the vessel was attacked and all those on board were killed. It was reported that Robert died on his knees whilst offering a Bible to one of the soldiers. Many copies of the Scriptures survived, however. Later, the soldier who had killed Robert became a Christian himself and was baptised, and several of his descendants became ministers of the gospel.

Understandably, Christian believers in Korea retained a deep sense of indebtedness to this young Welshman and the distant land from which he had come. Indeed, when the wind of revival swept across Korea in 1907 and Christian churches were so richly blessed by God, it was the hymns of Williams Pantycelyn that the people most loved to sing. Some impression of the extent of this and more recent revivals may be gained from what one of the visiting ministers told the present-day Mr Williams. When asked how many active members he had in his church, he replied, 'Six thousand'! I found myself asking what William Williams would have made of that. There is certainly no doubt whatsoever that he felt just as passionately as Robert Thomas about preaching the gospel overseas. It is said that Selina, Countess of Huntingdon, asked him to write a missionary hymn, and that it was probably as he was travelling to the Rhondda and saw the hills shrouded in storm clouds that he was moved to write:

> O'er the gloomy hills of darkness
>   Look, my soul; be still and gaze;
> All the promises do travail
>   With a glorious day of grace:
>   Blessèd Jubilee!
>   Let thy glorious morning dawn.
>
> Kingdoms wide that sit in darkness,
>   Grant them, Lord, Thy glorious light;
> And from eastern coast to western
>   May the morning chase the night;
>   And redemption,
>   Freely purchased, win the day.

It was not easy to take my leave of this very special place. But there was farm work demanding the attention of Mr Williams, and I had to resume my journey.

The walk back to Llandovery was saved from being an anticlimax by an unexpected encounter in a lay-by a mile from the town. I had stopped at a mobile snack bar and was thoroughly enjoying a sausage, bacon and egg sandwich and a mug of tea, the sheer good value of which was reflected in the steady stream of drivers who were obviously in the habit of stopping here for lunch. Among the parked vehicles stood a pick-up truck with a sign of a fish on the tailboard. It did not take me long to find the owner among the other drivers, and as soon as I mentioned the fish, he told me that his name was Anthony and that he was a committed Christian. The secret symbol adopted by believers in Roman times still enables Christians to recognise each other today.

Over a second mug of tea, Anthony told me that he was a gypsy, married with four teenage children and living in Llandovery. Before he became a Christian he used to visit fairs, where he would compete in the boxing ring as a prize-fighter. Even as we talked, I could well imagine him in that role. All that now belonged to the past, however, and since putting his faith in Christ his life had changed radically. Indeed, recognising that he had specific gifts, a local church had appointed him as a Christian worker among travelling people —a ministry he seemed admirably suited to fulfil. It was good to be able to pray together before we separated, even though we were to meet again. He arrived at the campsite later that evening and insisted on taking me to his home for a meal with his wife and family!

Distance walked: 7 miles. (Total 152 miles.)

*   *   *   *   *   *   *

Next morning, I left Llandovery to continue my journey. By now the Black Mountain (or Mynydd Du) extended across the southern horizon, and I wanted to reach the campsite at Cross Inn, near Llanddeusant, that night. From there, a crossing of these hills the following day should be quite straightforward.

By now the weather seemed to be set fair, and as I climbed steadily out of the Tywi valley, the temperature climbed also. This six-mile section of my walk would follow lanes all the way, but these were by no means unpleasant, undulating between fragrant hedgerows and frequently giving expansive views across most attractive countryside.

I was very taken by the village of Myddfai, and recalled the story of its physicians. The tale describes how a young man who lived at Blaensawdde Farm (GR784239), near Llanddeusant, wooed and then wed a beautiful maiden he had met beside Llyn y Fan Fach. Before they were married, the girl made it known that she was decidedly different from other women, and that if he ever struck her three times, she would surely return to the waters of the lake from which she had come. They raised three sons before the 'strike rate' unfortunately reached three and, true to her word, she went from his life as mysteriously as she had entered it. The three sons diligently sought their mother and eventually found her one day by the lake and, from the frequent meetings that ensued, learnt from her much about the healing properties of many of the mountain herbs.

Many local physicians subsequently claimed to be descendants of the three sons, the last being a Dr Rice Williams of Aberystwyth, who died in 1842. Though clearly there is much that is mythical about the story, it would be rash to dismiss all the claims made by the 'physicians'. Indeed, as recently as 1999, students of pharmacology have been examining the properties of many of the ancient herbal extracts and recipes used by the medical men of Myddfai, and finding much that could be of great value to modern drug therapy.

In the porch of the attractive whitewashed parish church stands a tombstone inscribed:

Here lieth the body of Mr. David Jones of Mothvey
Surgeon, who was an honeſt, charitable & ſkillfull man.
He died Septmr ye 14th Anno Dom 1719 aged 61
John Jones, Surgeon, eldeſt son of the ſaid David Jones
departed this life the 25th of November 1739
in the 44th yeare of his age and alſo lyes Interred hereunder.

It would appear that the good people of this village were well catered for in these distant pre-NHS days! The only 'drug' of questionable value I imbibed that morning was a cup of coffee ordered at the Plough Inn—a picturesque oak-beamed building converted from an old barn. Whether it did me any good, who is to say, but it certainly left me feeling refreshed.

There are two roads between Myddfai and Cross Inn (GR773258), with little to choose between them in terms of distance or attractiveness. They are equally hilly, twisting and appealing to the senses. I opted for the more easterly of the two, but whichever one is followed, at the end a total of 600 feet will have been gained in height. It was still comparatively early when I reached Cross Inn, but it was already very hot. I therefore decided to stay, rest and save my energy for the following day.

The campsite also played a part in this decision, for it would have been difficult to find anywhere a location with a more impressive panoramic view of the Black Mountain. (This should be distinguished from the Black Mountains to the east of the Brecon Beacons.) The skyline is dominated by the twin summits of Picws Du and Fan Foel (2457 feet and 2631 feet respectively). On the far side, their southern slopes descend gradually over broken and marshy ground to the valley of Afon Tawe. But viewed from the north—and I pitched my tent to take full advantage of the spectacle—the escarpment drops steeply from what are collectively known as

Bannau Sir Gaer (or the Carmarthenshire Beacons) to the twin lakes of Llyn y Fan Fach and Llyn y Fan Fawr. As the afternoon turned to evening, and the sun moved steadily westward, so the horizontal lines of strata and vertical gullies, hardly discernible at midday, appeared etched in ever-deepening shadow.

After a satisfying supper I retired early to get a good night's rest. At about one o'clock in the morning I suddenly woke. The tent was suffused with an unearthly white light. I unzipped the doorway and peered out. A full moon had risen from behind Fan Foel, and was bathing the entire landscape in pure, bright light. It was breathtaking. It was also quite cold, so that by the time I had settled down again, I was wide awake and fearful that sleep might be slow to return. It soon did, however, but even with the return of morning light it was the memory of that moonlit landscape that was most indelibly impressed upon my mind.

Distance walked: 6 miles. (Total 158 miles.)

---

1   Written originally in Welsh and translated into English by Peter Williams (1723–96) with William Williams' involvement.
2   Elsie Houghton, *Christian Hymn-writers*, Bryntirion Press (1982), p. 113.
3   Translated from Welsh by Richard Morris Lewis (1847–1918).

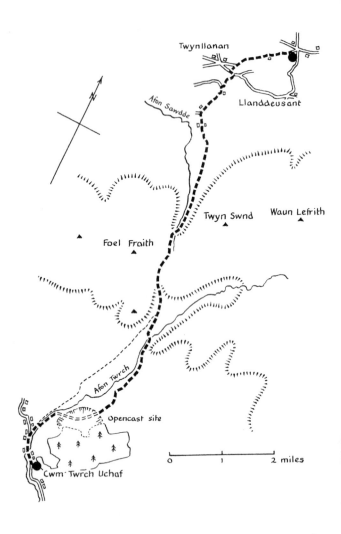

Twynllanan

Afon Sawdde

Llanddeusant

Waun Lefrith

Twyn Swnd

Foel Fraith

Afon Twrch

Opencast site

Cwm Twrch Uchaf

0   1   2 miles

17
Black mountain, bleak landscape

After several days spent walking along leafy lanes (let's forget the A40!) and following river valleys, however delightful, I was by now looking forward to being once more 'upon high places'. My main concern was the heat, for today's route would offer little in the way of shade, and at eight-thirty, as I set off, the strength of the sun was already noticeable. From Cross Inn the narrow road ran south-west toward Twynllannan, but a few hundred yards before the village I followed a footpath across the fields and down to a lane which crossed Afon Sawdde and began the climb up to Tŷ Brych farm.

It was getting warmer by the minute and, as the dogs greeted my approach, I decided to ask if I could top up my water containers from an outside tap. Farmer Bryn Price came out of the house to see what all the commotion was about. He told me that few walkers approached the tops by this route, and that his dogs were unaccustomed to strangers passing that way. He assured me that I was welcome, nonetheless, as his wife Elaine came out to join him. She had only stayed back to put the kettle on! A charming Yorkshire lady, Elaine had married Bryn five years earlier, some time after the death of his first wife, and had come to share her life with him in this remote place. When I told them that I had a son named Bryn and a wife called Elaine, there was immediately a rapport between us. Sitting in the cool of their front room, we spoke together of loneliness, the crisis in the livestock industry, of bereavement and the value of true faith in a living God. After a second cup of tea and several pieces of shortbread, I reluctantly left my two new friends and began the climb up Cwm Sawdde Fechan in earnest.

As I had already found on previous occasions, the path is far more obvious on the map than it was on the ground. Visibility was excellent, however, and the terrain made for fairly easy walking. I therefore made directly for the saddle between Foel Fraith and Esgair Hir. In poor weather this would be bleak country indeed. From Sawdde Fechan, the small stream below me, unbroken grassy slopes void of any distinguishing features rose to more than 2000 feet. Lower down, an occasional stunted rowan tree struggled for survival in the peat soil, but above 1000 feet nothing but a few ferns growing beside the stream interrupted the endless sweep of grass and rushes. And yet here was beauty to behold. As the morning wore on and I approached the *bwlch*, small patches of cumulus cloud cast their patchwork shadows on the surrounding slopes, their subtle shades of green, brown and ochre forever changing. In a poem entitled 'The Moor', the frequently mystical R. S. Thomas writes of such places:

> It was like a church to me.
> I entered it on soft foot,
> Breath held like a cap in the hand.
> It was quiet.

Quiet, most surely. Yet God was there, and in the beauty of the colours and the breath of the wind I could see reflected his beauty and sense his breath, and I worshipped not creation but him as Creator.

I reached the *bwlch* (GR765185) at midday precisely and 'refuelled' on oatcakes, butter and honey. At 1673 feet this was the watershed between two contrasting worlds. To the north lay a pastoral landscape of secret valleys and green fields speckled with sheep, whose population dwelt in tiny villages and isolated farms. To the south, as yet unseen but awaiting me, the terraced cottages and abandoned pits of the Tawe, Neath and Ely valleys—a world of industry old and new, of rugby clubs and male voice choirs and close-knit communities. There can surely be no place in Wales where the transition from one environment to another is so marked. But before I could appreciate fully the contrast, I must descend from these heights, and that was to be not nearly as simple as I anticipated.

My intention was straightforward enough: head south with Cefn Carn Fadog on my right, following the line of a footpath marked on the OS map down to Afon Twrch (GR772162), and then along the east bank of the river to Cwm-twrch Uchaf. Anyone inclined to make the same crossing of these hills would, I feel, be better advised to use the bridleway that traverses the steep slope of Pen yr Helyg to the west of the river, and then descends south-south-west to meet a track at GR760141, just a mile north-east of Cwmllynfell.

I reached and crossed Afon Twrch as planned, and enjoyed the company of the river. Small trout darted to and fro in the crystal-clear water. It was still very warm, and I rested awhile beside a small pool some yards from the river and at the very foot of a steep, grassy slope. Although the surface of the water was perfectly still, the light-coloured gravel on the bottom was subject to great turbulence, as if some subterranean fire were heating it and causing it to boil vigorously. Far from being hot, however, the water was ice-cold. This was limestone country. The famous Dan-yr-ogof caves were but four miles to the east, and I was sitting by a spring whose water had percolated down through hundreds of feet of porous rock and was now bubbling to the surface. I drank deeply from the pure and so refreshing water. My feet were also in need of refreshment, but I was unable to keep them immersed for more than half a minute before they became numb with cold. I recalled a similar spring at the foot of the South Downs in Sussex, where upon a stone had been engraved words from Psalm 104:

> He sends the springs into the valleys;
> They flow among the hills . . .
> O LORD, how manifold are Your works!
> In wisdom You have made them all.
> (verses 10,24 New King James Version)

Thus invigorated, I continued on my way.

Approaching the waterfall marked on the map (GR773155), I was forced by a gorge to leave the river and climb a steep, bracken-covered slope to the derelict homestead of Dorwen. From there a well-defined track appeared to lead firstly south and then south-west back to the river above Ystradowen. Soon, however, I ran into difficulty. Quite suddenly, and with no indication of any such feature on the latest edition of the OS map, the road (along which it would have been possible to drive a motor vehicle) ended. Five large stones had been used to block the way, and I found myself standing on the edge of a vast man-made depression, a legacy of opencast mining. Away in the distance, what at first appeared to be a row of terraced houses turned out to be a fleet of giant 'Tonka' toy lorries parked in a line, each with wheels some eight feet in diameter. There was no sign of any diversionary path, either to the right or left, which might lead around this devastated, lunar-like landscape, and the thought of retracing my steps two miles up the valley never entered my head.

By now I was beginning to feel weary. My judgement was possibly impaired also, as a result of the heat and dehydration. Rightly or wrongly, I calculated that my most direct route lay directly across this unfenced and seemingly open area, and that I would be able to walk to the other side and reach Ystradowen. At no point was the 'pit' excessively deep, and it was quite easy to walk down an incline of some fifty feet to the excavated floor. However, even at that depth below the level of the surrounding countryside, I at once lost sight of any identifiable landmarks, and was compelled to use my compass to navigate a circuitous route around slurry pits and across extensive areas of blasted rock and hard-baked, rutted mud. Furthermore, in this albeit shallow depression excavated in man's quest for cheap coal, the heat of the sun was intensified. It not only shone down from above, but was also reflected from the sides and floor of the workings. Almost all my water had been used up. The entire area had an air of abandonment about it. I suddenly felt rather vulnerable. To collapse from heat exhaustion in such a place on a Saturday afternoon was not something I wished to contemplate!

I have never been one to take unnecessary risk or venture into situations of known danger or difficulty, in the belief that if I got myself into trouble God would get me out. There are people—members of the rescue services, for example—who may be called upon to put their own lives at risk in order to save others, and we greatly admire their courage. That is one thing. But needlessly to imperil oneself in recreational or non-essential activity, trusting that God will take care of you, is another thing altogether. To my mind, it flies in the face of personal responsibility and reduces God to some kind of insurance policy. I had, at the start of the day, certainly committed myself into God's hands and asked him to guard both myself and those I loved, but this did not give me an excuse to cut corners, take risks or act in a careless manner. There may well have been mistakes made which led to my being in that worrying situation—navigational errors or a failure to recognise an easier route—I accept that, for those are things we are all prone to. What I had not done, however, was to place myself in danger knowingly and needlessly. Without any hesitation or embarrassment, therefore, I asked God for his guidance and strength. I may not have been 'lost' exactly, but I certainly did not know which direction to take in order to find a safe and convenient way out. I also had enough awareness to realise that I was suffering from dehydration and heat exhaustion. Furthermore, whilst getting out of this hostile environment was my immediate priority, there was also the need to find somewhere suitable to camp that night. With all these things in mind, very simply I sought God's help. He was, after all, my heavenly Father. It seemed an obvious and appropriate thing to do in the circumstances.

Suddenly, from somewhere down in the valley away to my right, I heard the distant sound of children's voices. With a sense of great relief I set off in that direction; scrambled up a slope of loose rock; somehow found enough energy to negotiate a barbed-wire fence, and then slithered through bushes down an embankment to the river. The children playing in the water below the weir stopped their splashing and stood looking in wide-eyed astonishment as this bearded old man (old, at least, in their eyes!) with a rucksack on his back careered down the grass on his bottom! An understandably protective mother stood guard over her charges. Her countenance soon softened when she heard my story, however, and she kindly directed me to the footpath that would take me down to the village. I was to discover later that this opencast site had been a most con-tentious issue with local people for more than three years, and that I was by no means the first to be completely confused by this development. A particularly frustrating experience, and one which hopefully others will avoid by keeping to the hills west of the river.

Reaching the main road that ran through the village, I turned left and began to walk down the hill. I urgently needed to obtain some fresh water, but as it was the weekend there were few people around. I had already gone to one house where an elderly lady was tending her front garden, but seeing me approach she had hurried inside and closed the door. I guess I must have looked rather dishevelled, and so I could hardly blame her.

Then, set back a little from the street, I noticed an attractive terrace of three cottages, the front door of one of which stood open. I knocked and a tall, kindly gentleman answered. Yes, of course I could have some water, he told me, and took my bottle from me. Then his wife appeared, and immediately insisted that I came in and sat down. She seemed anxious, and yet acted with an air of authority. I was to sit quietly while she made me a cup of sweetened tea—and then another, followed by a third. Joan, Ted's wife (both of whom were in their eighties, though few would have known it), had been a nurse. Not until the following morning did she tell me how concerned she had been. It seems as though I had stood in their doorway showing all the classic symptoms of heat exhaustion, and having the appearance of someone quite ill. I cheekily told her that I thought she was exaggerating, but calling to mind the experience of the young man I had met on Pumlumon, whose first attempt to walk this route had ended at Machynlleth due to heatstroke, I am not too sure. I shall certainly always be grateful for their kindness. Numerous cups of tea were followed by a meal, and then by the suggestion that I sleep that night in their spare room. Any argument on my part that I really didn't want to be a nuisance was probably somewhat muted. This, I was sure, was God's provision, and after walking so much of the way on my own I really did enjoy their company. Ted had served in World War II with the Royal Marine Commandos;

149

then in the CID, and finally as head of security at Ford's Dagenham factory. A big man, and strong in spite of his eighty-plus years, I suspect he was confident that he could deal with any threat I might pose!

Ted and Joan also had links with the church I very much wanted to attend the following morning. Before ever setting out on this journey I had already heard from a number of people about the Tro'r Glien Mission Hall in Cwm-twrch. The church had come into existence in the aftermath of the 1904 Revival, and had a quite remarkable history. Now, it looked as if my hope of visiting the church on a Sunday was about to be fulfilled, thanks to those who were ready and willing to welcome into their home one who was a complete stranger.

Distance walked: 11 miles. (Total 169 miles.)

---

1   R. S. Thomas, op. cit., p. 88.

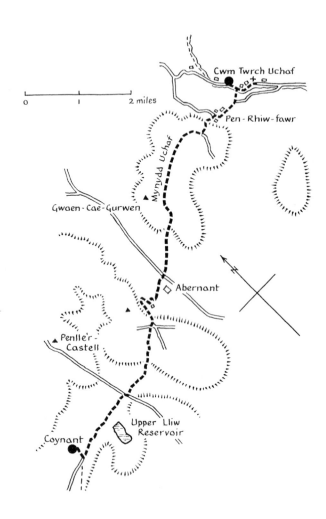

Cwm Twrch Uchaf

Pen-Rhiw-fawr

Mynydd Uchaf

Gwaen-Cae-Gurwen

Abernant

Penlle'r-
Castell

Upper Lliw
Reservoir

Coynant

0   1   2 miles

18
Valleys not so green

On Thursday 29 September 1904, two ministers, the Revds Seth Joshua and Joseph Jenkins, together with a former miner recently accepted as a candidate for the ministry named Evan Roberts, met for a Christian conference in the village of Blaenannerch, four miles north-east of Cardigan. What occurred was to have a remarkable effect upon the whole of Wales in the months that were to follow. Each of the three individuals had been deeply concerned about the weakened state of the churches across the land, and the lack of vision and power in the ministry of those churches. Each of them had long been pleading with God in prayer, asking that he would come in might by his Spirit, and deal with the apathy, worldliness and doctrinal error that were responsible for this rapid decline into spiritual oblivion. Each had also seen evidence of God blessing their own ministries in various parts of Wales, with many coming to faith in Christ under their preaching. But it was not until these three men met in this unpretentious Cardiganshire village that God in his grace came upon them in the way they had so desired.

It is the name of the third man, Evan Roberts, the ex-miner and blacksmith from Loughor, that is most often associated with the 1904–5 revival. And when I reached Loughor the following day I was to learn more about this young man of just 26 years who was so remarkably used by God. I have simply introduced the events of the autumn of 1904 at this point in my journey, because the church in Cwm-twrch that I planned to attend that morning came into being as a direct result of these happenings.

The revival itself lasted less than a year, but not before a number of people from various churches in Cwm-twrch had been deeply affected. Concerned that not enough was being done for the many poor families in the community, most of whom were too embarrassed by their illiteracy and lack of smart clothes to attend the 'respectable' chapels of the village, a Sunday school was started. Here initially the children, but subsequently their parents also, could learn to read the Bible and receive instruction in the Christian faith. Very sadly, the church with which most of these workers were associated disapproved of this new venture and, after a short while, asked those concerned to resign their membership and leave the church. God so encouraged them in this pioneering work, however, that before long they were able to secure a site in a strategic position and build their own meeting place. Thus the Tro'r Glien Mission Hall came into being. During the Christmas holidays of 1912, it was decided to hold a series of meetings over a four-day period, at which Stephen Jeffreys, a miner from Maesteg, was invited to preach. Such was the anointing of God upon Jeffreys' preaching and the pouring out of his Spirit upon these meetings that they continued for seven weeks without a break. A great many people were brought into a personal relationship with Christ during that time, most of whom were baptised in Afon Twrch, which flowed through the village. Jeffreys never returned to his job as a miner. He spent the rest of his life preaching the gospel of Christ.

What had happened in Cwm-twrch can only be understood in terms of revival in a fairly small and clearly defined area. This was to occur on other occasions and in several different locations across Wales, for quite a while after the nationwide 1904–5 revival had ended. I was therefore eager to visit a church fellowship that had come into existence in such a remarkable way, and to meet those who were still maintaining a witness in the same place, ninety years later.

The Mission Hall was easily located and, leaving my rucksack in the vestibule, I joined the small group of worshippers. It was a school holiday week, so several families were absent, but I was made most welcome and was asked many questions once the service was over. They were clearly not accustomed to have anyone walk 175 miles to attend one of their meetings, and they kindly wished me God's blessing as I went on my way refreshed in both body and spirit.

Crossing the river, I left Cwm-twrch Uchaf by means of a flight of concrete steps ascending through the woods from the main road up to the village of Penrhiw-fawr. The village street also continued steeply upward, and I was so grateful when a friendly milkman unloading his delivery van offered me a bottle of ice-cold milk to drink. There was more cloud today, and I was spared the direct rays of the sun, but it was still very warm and I was anxious not to repeat the mistakes of the previous day and once more become dehydrated.

From the village a track leads south-west along the ridge of Mynydd Uchaf. Looking back, the awful scar of the opencast mine on the far side of the valley that had been the scene of yesterday's adventure was clearly visible. Once again I was struck by the sheer scale of the workings and the amount of earth and rock that had been excavated—spoil that had been heaped up and partially grassed over to form a small range of man-made hills to one side of the pit. Unfortunately, on Mynydd Uchaf one is not spared further despoiling of the natural landscape, even when the back has been turned on the opencast workings above Ystradowen. On the ridge itself are discarded tyres, a burnt-out motor vehicle, household rubbish spilling from black plastic bags, and coils of rusting wire hidden in the grass to trip the unwary. Away to the north, between Tairgwaith and Brynaman, there is yet more opencast activity. The existence of this site is at least acknowledged by the Ordnance Survey, with footpaths and contour lines mysteriously finishing on the edge of a mile-wide area of white 'nothingness' on the map. Descending on a tarmac road and crossing the A474 (GR703086) brings little in the way of improvement. The once bustling Abernant colliery, providing employment for so many men, now stands silent, with only the memory of those who once lived, and sometimes died, extracting anthracite from the seams deep beneath the Upper Clydach valley. I walked on, perplexed and saddened. The inevitable signs, even scars, of industry I could accept. Of course we need our railway system and factories. I keep warm in winter by burning anthracite, and that can only come from a mine, and preferably a British mine. But when an opencast pit is worked out or found to be unproductive, or a factory becomes uneconomical and is forced to close—or an obsolete nuclear power station in Snowdonia can no longer safely generate electricity, come to that!—why, oh why, are these sites simply left to decay and disfigure the countryside for years to come? There is no shortage of finance when these projects are developed. Why should economics be the excuse for simply leaving them to rust once they have served their purpose?

Climbing the hill toward Pwllwatkin farm, one may as well forget green pastures and contented sheep. This is now a vast landfill site, the obnoxious smell of which reaches you on the wind when still half a mile away. Sunday afternoon 'rubbish dumpers' drove past with their broken refrigerators and cardboard boxes of waste, to be greeted by thousands of gulls who, for some reason I cannot begin to understand, seemed to prefer this environment to the glorious coastline of the Gower! At the side of the road that followed the perimeter fence, black oily ooze seeped from the nettle-covered bank and ran down a nearby drain. Whatever are we doing to this beautiful world God has given us not only to inhabit, but also to care for? I am not one who would put the welfare of animals or the environment before either the material or spiritual needs of individuals, but I do believe as a Christian that God expects me to appreciate and act responsibly as a 'care-taker' of all that he has created.

Above Pwllwatkin farm the road zigzagged up the bracken-clad hillside to a shallow saddle between Bryn Mawr and Mynydd Carnllechart. At almost 1000 feet the air was worth breathing again, and those sights and smells that had offended the senses earlier were now thankfully left behind. A rough track took me down to Nant Moel farm and the Lower Clydach valley. A chapel stood silhouetted on the skyline. I wondered at the circumstances that prompted the building of a place of worship in such an isolated and at times inhospitable place; I thought of the remote homesteads it had served, and of the changes it must have witnessed through all the years it had stood there. It must surely have been a place of such lonely dereliction that moved R. S. Thomas, in a poem entitled 'The Chapel', to write these lines:

> But here once on an evening like this,
> in the darkness that was about
> his hearers, a preacher caught fire
> and burned steadily before them
> with a strange light, so that they saw
> the splendour of the barren mountains
> about them and sang their amens
> fiercely, narrow but saved
> in a way that men are not now.

The windows of the farm kitchen were open, and someone called to me as I crossed the yard. I needed fresh water, so welcomed the friendly greeting. Three generations were still sitting around a well-scrubbed table and the sink was piled high with dirty dishes. At three o'clock they had finished eating, but tea was flowing freely and I was soon perched on the windowsill with a large steaming mug in my hand. We chatted for a while. Water bottles were filled, and I was pointed in the right direction.

Down in the valley the stream sparkled with patches of sunlight that filtered through the foliage. Below a narrow footbridge, mosses and ferns grew in rich profusion from water-worn terraces of rock. Birds sang. Here there was no waste or vandalism to dispirit. Men passed this way. Tractor tyres had left their imprint in the mud where a farm track crossed the brook. But I knew, from the conversation I had enjoyed at the farm, that these were people who valued the beauty that surrounded them and sought to preserve it for those who would come after them.

Climbing out of this tranquil valley, I crossed the road that runs between Ammanford and Clydach, and headed westward over the trackless golden grassy moorland of Mynydd y Gwair. To the south, sheltered by a spruce plantation, the waters of the Upper Lliw reservoir were deep blue in the late afternoon sunshine. Before dropping down into yet another steep-sided valley that cradled the infant Afon Lliw, I paused to check my bearing with map and compass. Ceunant farm, my destination for that day, was less than a mile away, but that also lay concealed in the next fold of the hills, and I wanted to cross the ridge between Mynydd y Gwair and Mynydd Garn-fach at the right place. Thus reassured, it was over the stream and up the hillside to join a farm track that contoured around the northern slopes of Mynydd Garn-fach. I did not realise it at the time, but this short climb was to be the very last ascent of the entire journey. Tomorrow it was to be downhill all the way to the Loughor estuary!

Ceunant is rather different from your average Welsh hill farm. I was met at the gate by two black Australian swans, whilst from an enclosure near the house a pink flamingo 'trumpeted' my arrival. Later on I made the acquaintance of a pair of rare monkeys. But it was primarily the prospect of a comfortable bed and a welcome meal that had brought me to this delightful place, not to mention a much-needed shower before I reached civilisation the next day. Collecting my final food parcel, and preparing all that I would require for a prompt start next morning, I retired for the night.

Comfortable though the bed was, it was a while before I fell asleep. The end of my journey was in sight and my emotions were strangely confused. An understandable sense of achievement, together with relief that I would soon be giving my feet a well-earned rest, not to mention the eagerly anticipated reunion with my wife—these natural sentiments were mixed with a feeling not far removed from disappointment that my adventure was almost over. I had become accustomed to this uncomplicated lifestyle. There had been many occasions when I had been wet and weary, but for almost three weeks life had been lived on the basis of bare necessities. A satisfying meal, a few square feet of grass on which to pitch a tent, strength for the day's walk, and very occasionally the will to overcome unexpected obstacles and a determination to survive. But above all, I had been privileged to know a sense of God's presence uninterrupted by the 'busyness' of daily routine, and the all-too-common claims upon time and attention that clutter up our sophisticated lives. So frequently it is such that prevent us from hearing that still, small voice of divine reason and reassurance. Hopefully I would have learned something from this journey that I would be able to take with me back into what we must all accept as 'normal' life.

Distance walked: 11 miles. (Total 180 miles.)

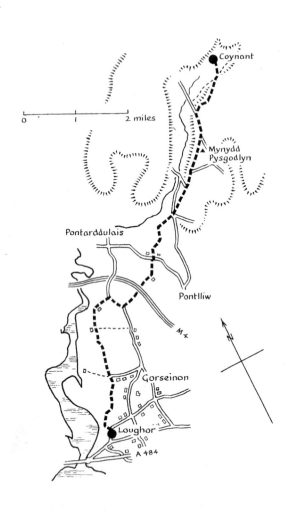

Coynant

Mynydd
Pysgodlyn

0   1   2 miles

Pontarddulais

Pontlliw

Mx

Gorseinon

Loughor

A 484

N

The view northwards toward Cadair Idris from near the summit of Pumlumon. Llyn Llygad Rheidol, source of the Afon Rheidol, lies immediately below (ch. 11).

An idyllic place to camp at the end of a long day (ch. 12)

Afon Rhiwnant between Elan Village and Abergwesyn (ch. 13).

Pantycelyn, formerly the home of the hymnwriter, William Williams (ch. 16).

Llandovery (ch. 15).

Bannau Sir Gaer, the Black Mountain, from Cross Inn (ch. 16).

The view northwards toward Llandovery and Pantycelyn down the Cwm Sawdde Fechan from the Black Mountain (ch. 17).

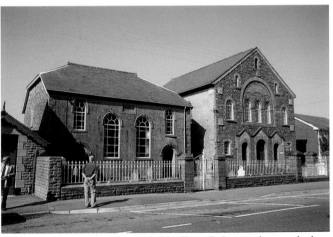

Capel Moriah, the chapel attended by Evan Roberts, where revival began in November 1904 (ch. 19).

19
Sea views and saltings

Suddenly the unlatched bedroom window blew wide open with a crash, and the curtains flapped wildly. I awoke with a start and stumbled out of bed. In the first grey light of an overcast dawn I could see the trees bending before the rising wind. Closing the window, I went back to bed. The sun had set under a clear sky the previous evening, and the forecast had been fairly good for what was to be my last full day of walking. Hopefully this squall would prove to be just a temporary 'interruption' in what was a most welcome spell of good weather.

For the second time on my journey, a night spent in a comfortable bed was followed by the kind of cooked breakfast for which the British are justly famous. That such a meal provides plenty of calories for a hard day's walking there can be little doubt. But I have never been one to rise in the morning, wash and dress, and immediately sit down to an overflowing plate of sausage, bacon, black pudding, egg, mushroom, tomato and baked beans! Perhaps if I were to try it more often? On second thoughts, maybe not. To eat small amounts of food on a more frequent basis seems to make more sense, and better serves both my metabolism and waist measurement.

Leaving Ceunant farm, the path led in a south-westerly direction contouring across the slopes of Mynydd Garn-fach. The hillside dropped away steeply on the right down to the woods and farmsteads of Cwm Dulais, but by keeping to the higher ground it was possible to follow the broad ridge to

161

Pysgodlyn (860 feet). Here there is no summit worthy of the name, and once again easy access by road has resulted in the inevitable dumping of rubbish. Indeed, on the highest point a beacon had been kindled a year or so before; one of a nation-wide network of bonfires intended to highlight the concern of country dwellers who perceived proposed government legisla-tion as a threat to their way of life. Sadly, their cause can hardly have been helped by the quantity of drink bottles and cans that still littered the ground even after such a length of time. Perhaps, one day soon, those who claim to care about the countryside will set an example by organising a 'clean-up' operation. This is certainly a beautiful area and well worth preserving, not least because of the close proximity of Penlle'r Bebyll—earthworks marking the site of a dwelling or fortifi-cation, which possibly date from the Iron Age.

For me, however, it was the sight of the sea that stirred my heart that morning. Apart from occasional glimpses of far-off Cardigan Bay from the hills of North Wales and Pumlumon, I had not seen the sea since leaving Llanfairfechan. Now, twenty days after turning my back on the Irish Sea, I found myself looking down the Bristol Channel to the Atlantic. I may have suffered slight tendonitis in my left leg and devel-oped a corn on my right little toe along the way, but in that special moment nothing was going to stop me completing my journey 'from shore to shore'! From the top of Pysgodlyn it is possible to follow the road south, down to the village of Felindre. My destination was Loughor, however, and with the M4 to cross I planned to keep to the lanes south-west along the ridge above Cwm Dulais, over the A48 and the railway line, and under the motorway at GR599019. This route avoids areas of urban development, and is a wise choice for another reason. Midway between the A48 and the M4, the Pontarddulais Garden Centre and Tea Rooms are to be found (GR604021), and whilst bedding plants or potting compost will be of little interest to the long-distance walker, the fare served in the Tea Rooms can be wholeheartedly recommended. Not only were their salmon sandwiches delicious, but when I was unable to eat all that they had set before me (due, no doubt, to the cooked breakfast), they even provided some 'cling-film' wrapper so that I could conveniently carry the remainder with me!

Soon after passing under the motorway, the B4296 is reached. By turning right to Waun-gron and taking the first minor road on the left, it is possible to reach the salt marshes that border the upper reaches of the Loughor estuary at Llwynadam farm. The path leading south across the marshes proved very pleasant. By now the sun had dispersed the low cloud of early morning and the strong wind had dropped. Beyond Grove farm, the right of way marked on the map became indistinct and appeared to have been fenced off, but by walking towards the estuary and Cwrt-y-carne farm, it was possible to follow the lane south-east and rejoin the original footpath before reaching Gorseinon (GR580999).

In spite of the nearness of the town, the rural nature of this route is maintained right into Loughor. Indeed, approaching Loughor from this rather unusual direction means that among the very first buildings encountered are two that were closely associated with the spiritual movement for which the place is best known, and the reason I wanted to visit it on my journey. Island House was the home of Evan Roberts, whilst Pisgah, the small chapel just around the corner, was the place of worship he attended as a young man.

It was three o'clock in the afternoon, and I was not expecting to meet Kevin until four-thirty. Resting in the shade outside The Reverend James public house, I read awhile and awaited the arrival of my friend. Intrigued by the name, I enquired concerning the identity of this man 'of the cloth' whose portrait now adorned an inn sign. His story was told in a framed manuscript just inside the entrance. He was, I was surprised to learn, a contemporary and close friend of Charles Wesley, who very nearly drowned whilst attempting to cross the Loughor estuary on his way to a preaching engagement. It appears that he had been given inaccurate instructions concerning the only safe route through the quicksands. He escaped with his life, however, and not only preached as planned, but some while later married into the Buckley family, of brewing fame. And I always believed the Methodists to be strong on temperance! I was more than happy with my iced ginger beer.

Arrangements had been made for me to spend the night in the home of Mike and Audrey. Kevin, Mike and Derrick Adams (the minister of my own home church in Penrhyndeudraeth) are brothers who grew up in Llanelli, just across the river from Loughor. Kevin especially has made a detailed study of the 1904–5 revival, and I could not have had a more helpful and competent mentor in my quest to learn more about the life and work of Evan Roberts. After visiting Moriah Chapel with its striking memorial to its best-known son in the forecourt, we retired to Kevin's study to examine numerous items of memorabilia and albums of yellowing press cuttings, and so I gained a detailed and graphic insight into the remarkable events of that period.

When Evan Roberts left Newcastle Emlyn on Monday 31 October 1904, to travel by train back to his home in Loughor, he did so with a sense of ever-increasing excitement and anticipation. At Blaenannerch he had experienced God working in a totally new and powerful way in his life, and now firmly believed that what had happened to him and his two friends, Seth Joshua and Joseph Jenkins, would in turn flow out to touch many more lives right across Wales. His first priority, however, was to return to Loughor and share all that had occurred with the young people of his own home church. At first his immediate family and close friends were troubled by the excitable manner and extravagant claims of this twenty-six-year-old young man. He seemed unable to explain to their satisfaction why he had so suddenly abandoned his studies or how he expected to be used by God. Nevertheless, the minister in charge at Moriah and the associated work at Pisgah allowed him to arrange a series of youth meetings. At first the young people were rather unresponsive, and seemed reluctant to make the public commitment to Christ for which Roberts had hoped and prayed. Undeterred, he continued with the meetings, seeing himself engaged in a spiritual battle for the souls of these young men and women. And it was not long before they recognised that the great concern being expressed by this man of fire, who now pleaded with them, actually reflected the far greater concern and compassion of the God who had sent him. One by one they openly confessed their sin, and sought forgiveness from Christ and the fullness of the Holy Spirit.

News of what was happening spread quickly. Earlier fears and suspicions were set aside, as his family and fellow church members now recognised that what was taking place in their church must surely be a work of God, and rejoiced accordingly. Invitations to conduct other meetings followed, and soon leaders of churches in neighbouring areas were seeking his help, in the hope that this season of spiritual awakening and blessing might also spread to their locality.

The nature of the meetings that took place and the rapid spread of this revival have been well documented (e.g. *The Welsh Revival of 1904* by Eifion Evans published by Bryntirion Press). Services often lasted into the small hours, and were characterised by spontaneity and great emotion as people

165

frequently wept or cried out in distress. An extensive report of events appeared in the *Western Mail* as early as Saturday 12 November, and from then onwards media interest was considerable.

At the same time that Roberts was being so powerfully used in Loughor, similar happenings began to occur in other places, involving other men. Gorseinon, New Quay, Carmarthen, Tonypandy and Ammanford all witnessed great blessing. Seth Joshua and Joseph Jenkins were both actively engaged in many of these places. In Ammanford bookshops quickly ran out of Bibles. Public houses stood largely empty as former patrons now sang, prayed and read the Scriptures with their families. Remarkable conversions bore witness to the power of God. Returning to his home for the Christmas vacation, one Cardiff student listened with amazement to the open-air preaching of one local man whose notoriety and ungodliness were widely known. He wrote at the time:

> At the square that night I joined a crowd listening to some-one speak from a platform. When I saw who it was I could hardly believe my eyes, for I knew him well, and everyone else knew him to be one of the profanest characters in the area. There he was . . . with sentences and verses of Scripture pouring forth from his lips. I did not know the story of his conversion but I knew of the fluency and blas-phemy of his oaths previously. That sudden view of him, so fervently commending the salvation which is in Christ to the surrounding crowd, shook me.[1]

The effect of the revival upon local colliery workers was particularly noteworthy. Mine managers at the time spoke of the improved attendance, punctuality, co-operation and atti-tude of their workforce. Union disputes became rare, whilst a

Western Mail reporter, visiting one pit, described night-shift miners going underground half an hour early in order to read the Bible and pray together before commencing work. In North Wales, too, communities were soon experiencing the very same religious fervour and consequential transformation. On 9 December the *Caernarvon and Denbigh Herald* reported:

> The religious revival appears to be rapidly spreading throughout North Wales. Meetings are held practically at every town, and great enthusiasm prevails. In Bethesda, damaging rifts between workers and management caused by strike action in the Penrhyn Quarries, were healed. One local minister wrote: The policemen tell me that the public houses are nearly empty, the streets are quiet, and swearing is rarely heard. Things are easy for the policemen here now—I hope they have a glorious holiday, and the district is quite prepared to support them henceforth—for doing nothing![2]

Even David Lloyd-George MP, later to become Prime Minister, likened the revival to a mighty earthquake, and to a tornado sweeping the country, bringing far-reaching national and social changes. He referred to a public house in his constituency where the takings one Saturday evening totalled 4fid![3]

By the end of December 1904, it was estimated that 32,000 had been converted in South Wales alone, and that the influence of the revival had spread as far as Liverpool and London. In the months that followed, many notable Christian leaders from all over the world visited Wales, with the result that revival fires were kindled in different parts of Europe, Asia, Africa, India and Australasia. Missionary societies saw a marked increase in the number of those offering themselves for service overseas, whilst in Britain those whose lives had been truly touched by God continued to serve the churches through the dark years of World War I and beyond.

By the autumn of 1905, however, the revival itself had lost its momentum. Physical and mental exhaustion were now taking their toll of Evan Roberts, whilst criticism from certain churchmen and the press wounded him sorely. Increasingly he withdrew from public ministry, eventually to become something of a recluse. Of course there were aspects of this great movement that give rise to concern. There were spurious conversions, exaggerated claims and fervour that went to unhealthy extremes. Evan Roberts's own role in what should have been seen primarily as a work of God was grossly overstated by some, and the attention of the press, with their obsession with personalities and a 'good story', are largely to be blamed for this. But that which was inspired and empowered by the Spirit, and sought to glorify God, had a greater impact for good upon our country than possibly anything else that happened in the first half of the twentieth century. Would that today's secularism and ungodliness were to drive Christians to their knees in repentance and supplication, as it did in the early 1900s!

Distance walked: 9 miles. (Total 189 miles.)

1   Eifion Evans, *The Welsh Revival of 1904*, Third Edition, Bryntirion Press (1987), p. 105.
2   ibid., p. 110.
3   ibid., pp. 114-15.

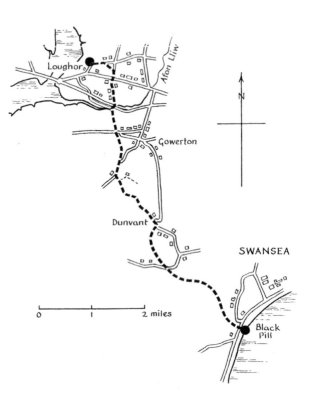

20
Journey's end

The morning dawned bright and fair for this, the last day and final leg of my journey. I had covered one hundred and ninety miles. Now there were but seven miles of pleasant, easy walking before I reached my ultimate goal. From the very beginning, and for most of the walk, I had deliberately put all thoughts of this day and its possible emotions out of my mind. I would not have been properly focused, nor would I have had the determination to persevere in the earlier stages, had I allowed myself to look ahead and envisage the joys and satisfaction of arrival. Today was different, however. Now I could smell the sea air. By midday I should be sitting on the beach gazing across Swansea Bay.

I was most grateful for the hospitality and support of my friends as I bade them a warm farewell. It was just eight o'clock when Kevin dropped me off at the apparently lifeless Reverend James. Commuters were already speeding to their places of work in Swansea, Llanelli and Ammanford as I navigated my way through the streets of Loughor, passing under the A484 and the Swansea to Carmarthen railway line, and over Afon Lliw (GR580972). When this journey 'from shore to shore' was first envisaged, I more or less accepted that the final day or two would take me unavoidably through industrial estates and areas of characterless urban sprawl. It goes without saying that I was totally unfamiliar with this part of West Glamorgan and could not have been more mistaken! A careful study of the map revealed numerous open spaces with small river valleys and scattered tracts of woodland linked by a network of connecting footpaths, each one an invitation to explore this area of rural tranquillity. Indeed, if the description that follows appears to be more detailed than some of the other sections which have preceded it, it has been done deliberately in the hope that others may perhaps enjoy the same pleasures by following in my footsteps.

Once the B4295 Gowerton to Pen-clawdd road has been crossed at GR581965, neither heavy traffic nor busy street will be met again until the coastal A4067 is crossed at Black Pill. From the traffic lights, a path immediately leads south-south-west into woodland, and at once I found myself in a delightful environment of sunlight and shade, mature trees and undergrowth, wild flowers and singing birds. Following a tiny stream that it crosses twice, the path continues on its western side, with very occasional glimpses of a new housing estate on the left. After approximately half a mile, a stile gives access to open pasture, beyond which runs a quiet lane (GR583957). Turning right and walking up the hill for a further half-mile, our route forks left opposite Cefn Golen Cottage in the direction of Gellyeithrym farm, and climbs gradually for 250 yards.

Care is needed at this point, for I almost missed the stile on the right that was overgrown by the thick hedge. Climbing the stile and keeping a fence on my right, I made my way through brambles and clumps of reed across a damp field to a gate and stile, beyond which lay the firmer ground of a farm track. Sitting on the stile, I watched a dog trotting towards me along the path and instinctively looked for its owner. It stopped, sat back on its haunches and regarded me quizzically. In response to my call it appeared to lose interest, rose and slowly sauntered off into a copse, displaying as it did so the rich red coat and full bushy tail of a healthy young vixen! I felt enormously privileged that she had not felt threatened by my presence and had drawn as close as she had, making this one of the high-lights of my day.

From the gate the track led past a small pond to a stile on the left. There seemed to be little evidence of any path leading from this through the copse beyond, but by scrambling up a bank to a further stile, easier ground was gained and followed eastwards along the side of a field. The route now drops down into a steeply sided valley, crossing four stiles on the way. Beyond the fourth, the path bears right following the valley bottom, with woodland on the left and a bracken-covered slope on the right. After just 50 yards, however, where the main path veers once more to the right, a less obvious track turns left into the woods, and may be followed with the assistance of orange waymarks to the road at Dunvant.

This contact with civilisation is short-lived. By turning left along the road and walking past Ebenezer Chapel and the children's playground, it is possible to join the Swansea Cycle Path, routed along the line of the former Mumbles Light Railway. The path has been tarmacked, but with only cyclists and pedestrians entitled to use it, it proved to be a delightful and easy three-mile walk along the Clyne Valley to the coast. Enclosed on both sides by trees, it affords few distant views, but since it was a hot day the shade was most welcome and the lakeside picnic site was a truly pleasant place to rest awhile. The growing noise of traffic signified that the path would soon end, but even so the sudden termination of my long journey came as something of a surprise. Emerging from shade into the bright sunshine, I was confronted by traffic lights controlling a pedestrian crossing and—on the far side of the road—the seashore! It was twelve noon precisely.

I walked between children with ice-cream-covered faces, whose parents (with sun-cream-covered bodies) viewed me with mild amusement. They wore only bathing costumes, with flip-flop sandals on their feet. I strode toward the sea wearing mountain boots and carrying a 35-pound rucksack on my back. Just one person's curiosity got the better of him. A distinguished-looking elderly gentleman with a white beard approached and asked me where I had come from. 'Llanfairfechan', I answered. 'Then allow me to be the official welcoming party', he replied, and shook me warmly by the hand. I readily admit to experiencing some difficulty in thanking him. I was already emotionally full.

For some days now I had been carrying in my rucksack a small, but nevertheless (by backpacking standards) rather heavy, tin of celebratory peaches. Sitting in the shade of a pine tree growing just above the beach, I opened it and relished, one by one, the golden, syrupy slices. Never had canned peaches tasted so good. How much I appreciated that dear man's kindly welcome! How much I enjoyed those peaches! But oh, how much more did I bless the One who had guided and provided, and brought me safely to my desired haven; the successful end of a memorable journey!

Boarding a bus, I travelled in comfort into Swansea city centre. A phone call home allowed me to share the news of my safe arrival with Elaine. Then it was on to Castle Street and the Café Continental, where I eagerly tucked into a generous portion of Welsh lamb with mint sauce and fresh vegetables. From my reading of the menu I was expecting to pay £4.95, but was handed a bill made out for £3.50. As I pointed out her mistake, the waitress smiled and told me that this was their normal discount for pensioners! 'Or long-distance walkers?' I enquired. 'Why not?' she replied.

The train took me to Whitland, where my son was waiting for me with his car. Then it was on to his home near Crymych, to be warmly greeted by his wife and two very excited grandchildren. The next day I would travel by bus via Aberystwyth and Machynlleth back to my own home and the very best welcome of all.

*   *   *   *   *   *   *

Many adventurers have undertaken far longer journeys and faced far greater dangers, in terrain infinitely more remote and challenging than anything I had traversed; but then this journey was never meant to test my endurance or skill to survive. I had walked almost two hundred miles to gain an overview of a land I had grown to love, and to meet people with whom I feel a great affinity. Although I cannot boast Welsh blood in my veins, nor do I possess the ability to speak the Welsh language as I would wish, my journeying had caused me to feel more than ever that this was where I belonged. Most significantly of all, as I considered its history and visited those places that had witnessed God's hand stretched out in such power and blessing, the words of Moses in Deuteronomy 11:11-12 seemed remarkably appropriate:

> The land you are crossing . . . is a land of mountains and valleys that drinks rain from heaven. It is a land the Lord your God cares for; the eyes of the Lord your God are continually on it from the beginning of the year to its end.

I had come to recognise the relevance of these words to this beautiful country and proud nation in which it was my privilege to dwell. May you, dear reader, acknowledge the same truth also.

Distance walked: 7 miles. (Total 196 miles.)

From all that dwell below the skies
Let the Creator's praise arise:
Let the Redeemer's Name be sung,
Through every land, by every tongue.

Eternal are Thy mercies, Lord;
Eternal truth attends Thy Word:
*Thy praise shall sound **from shore to shore**,*
Till suns shall rise and set no more.

Isaac Watts

Appendices

1. Route finding

It was never my intention that *From Shore to Shore* be used as a guidebook. However, it is to be hoped that some readers might be encouraged by this account to walk some or even all of the route for themselves. The following information is for their guidance.

A guidebook is a must, and the one I found most useful is *A Welsh Coast to Coast—Snowdonia to Gower* by John Gillham, published by Cicerone Press. Suitable maps are even more important. I used the Ordnance Survey 1:50,000 'Landranger' series. There is, of course, more detail on the 1:25,000 'Outdoor Leisure' series, but the number of sheets required and the cost would be considerable.

Six-figure grid references have been used extensively in the book, as the most convenient and widely recognised method of identifying a particular position on the map. For those unfamiliar with this system, instructions are to be found printed on all OS 'Landranger' maps. The maps required for the route described in this book are as follows:

Sheet 115	Snowdon
Sheet 124	Dolgellau
Sheet 135	Aberystwyth and Machynlleth
Sheet 147	Elan Valley and Builth Wells
Sheet 160	Brecon Beacons
Sheet 159	Swansea and Gower

A compass will also be required (and, of course, the skill to use it!).

The total distance of this journey was 196 miles covered in 20 days of walking. On two occasions I walked 16 miles in one day, which meant that on other occasions I covered less than ten miles. Much depends on age, fitness and experience, but an average of between ten and twelve miles per day will allow plenty of time for exploring, photography, conversation, eating and resting, whilst those who are fitter and more energetic should be able to complete the journey in two weeks.

2. Equipment

Clothing: From the account of this walk it will be appreciated that, even in summer, unseasonable weather may be encountered, particularly above 1500 feet. By using the widely accepted 'layering' system of clothing, however, all climatic conditions can be catered for.

A **base layer** of synthetic material will be quick-drying and will wick moisture caused by sweating away from the skin. Such garments are warm when used under other layers, but cool when worn on their own. Cotton is cool when dry, but during activity quickly becomes sweat-soaked and uncomfortable, and is slow to dry. On my walk I wore a Paramo reversible shirt which, though somewhat expensive, gives one the versatility of two garments in one—worn one way for warmth, it may be turned inside out when something cooler is required.

A **mid-layer** consisting of a lightweight fleece will provide warmth when the temperature drops, especially if it is worn under a windproof shell made of Pertex or similar closely woven fabric. I also carried a spare thermal vest to wear at night, but in very cold weather it could have been used as an additional layer. I tend not to take much in the way of spare clothing when trekking. Modern fabrics dry quickly, even if put on wet! My 'spares' are normally restricted to socks and underclothes, with other items being washed when necessary. An outer layer that is both waterproof and breathable is vital, and completes the system. With many 'state of the art' Gore-tex waterproof jackets costing £300, some may imagine that they will have to spend a great deal of money if they are to remain dry in the mountains. This is not true. Nor do a waterproof jacket or over-trousers need to be particularly heavy. Hopefully these will spend most of the time in your rucksack, so why carry more weight than you need to? On this walk I used a Craghopper 'Pakka' waterproof jacket which cost £35, and over-trousers made of the same Aqua Dry C proofed Pertex material (£30). These were more breathable than many waterproofs costing four times as much, and kept me perfectly dry on the twelve days out of twenty that I needed to wear them. Weight of both garments: 1 lb. 2 oz.

Footwear: Boots that provide good ankle support, and the cleated soles of which grip well on greasy rock or wet grass, are essential. For a long while now I have worn boots made by a German company, Meindle, finding them both supportive and comfortable from the very start. I began the walk wearing a pair of their light 'Borneo' boots, but switched to the 'Island Pro' when I felt I needed a boot with a higher ankle and waterproof membrane—the bogs in mid-Wales tended to be deeper than those in the north! People's feet differ enormously, and not just in shoe size. Find a model that suits, break them in, and then look after them—and they will look after you. Where stretches of road are likely to be encountered, a pair of sturdy trainers or trekking sandals makes a welcome change from heavier or more rigid boots.

Trekking poles: Once thought of as an aid for the infirm or elderly, the tremendous value of telescopic poles is now widely recognised, both by mountain walkers who are wise enough to use them, and by orthopaedic specialists, even before any medical condition may have manifested itself. Whether descending steep and rough terrain, balancing on boulders when crossing a stream, or using them to generate extra power when walking uphill, the difference they make is remarkable. Many doctors are now suggesting that the use of poles early on in one's walking career will protect against hip, knee and ankle problems in later life. I, certainly, would not want to walk far without my 'Khola' poles, and they can easily be strapped on the rucksack when they are not required. And yes—two are better than one. The use of only one pole can throw the body off balance and lead to problems with the back or shoulders.

Pack: The choice of a rucksack is almost as important, from the point of view of comfort and stability, as the choice of footwear. The amount you intend to carry will determine the type and size of pack selected, but comfort is paramount. Indeed, a slightly heavier or bigger model than you may think is really needed, with a well-padded back, shoulder straps and hip-belt, will be far more comfortable than a lightweight design where the straps cut into your shoulders, or any sharp objects being carried dig into your back. Remember, too, that back length differs from one person to another, and try to ensure that more weight is borne by the hips than by the shoulders.

Tent: Those who choose to undertake long walks and camp tend to be a rare breed, especially when, by using youth hostels or bed and breakfast accommodation, it is possible to carry a much lighter load. There is, however, a freedom afforded the backpacker or lightweight camper which a few of us really do delight in. The advice that follows is for those especially.

I walked this particular journey alone, even though my wife and I still enjoy walking and camping together. I therefore used a small, one-person 'Solar' tent made in Britain by Terra Nova. I have, in the past, also used a 'Microlight' made by Macpac of New Zealand, and currently have a Hilleberg 'Akto' manufactured in Sweden, which possibly stands up better to severe weather and therefore may be more suited to mountain use than the other two. All three tents weigh under 4 lb., and although none are cheap, looked after, they will last a very long time. If two are walking together, then although the weight of a larger tent will possibly be in the region of 6 lb. or more, this, together with other shared equipment such as stove, fuel and maps, etc., will be divided between two, and the weight carried by each will be significantly reduced. For solo walks, my rucksack and its contents weigh between 22 and 24 lb., before food and photographic equipment are added. Total weight would not normally exceed 35 lb. unless venturing into very remote, wilderness areas, where extra food and items of equipment are going to be required. Walking with a companion will reduce this to about 30 lb.

Sleeping bag and **Mat:** At my age I do enjoy a certain level of comfort, but this does not necessarily mean carrying items that are heavy or bulky. My three-season Rab down-filled sleeping bag has kept me warm when the temperature has fallen to -05°C in the Alps, yet weighs only 2 lb. 3 oz. Even the modern generation of much less expensive synthetic-filled bags turn in a similar performance for the same weight, though they may not pack down quite so small.

For a mattress, I abandoned the yellow Karrimat, still so popular with more hardy backpackers, many years ago. The range of self-inflating mats made by Thermarest provide just as much insulation from the cold ground, but with a much greater degree of comfort. More expensive than foam mats, certainly, but a pair of standard Thermarest mats we purchased 25 years ago are still in use, in spite of the repair patches with which they are adorned. Weight: 1 lb. 3 oz.

Cooking: Over the years I have cooked using several different fuels. Methylated spirit, paraffin, petrol and gas all have pros and cons. Increasingly these days, and for this journey in particular, I chose to use gas. It is clean, convenient and relatively safe if the weather necessitates cooking under the cover of a flysheet. It is also by now widely available.

The main drawback is still the reluctance of different producers—notably Camping Gaz, Epigas, Coleman and Primus, to standardise the fitting by which stoves are attached to their various cartridges (even though the first three named are now owned by the same company). However, a relatively new British company, Go Gas, has produced a very useful adapter. This enables the widely available Camping Gaz C 206 cartridges which, once pierced, had to remain attached to the stove until it was empty, to be used with other makes of stove fitted with a screw-thread attachment. This now allows stove and cartridge to be dismantled and packed separately, or a nearly exhausted cartridge with low gas pressure to be kept just for simmering. With such an adapter it is now possible to use almost any brand of butane/propane mix that is available—a tremendous advantage. All of my cooking was done using a tiny Coleman 'Micro' stove weighing just 6 oz. and two pans (0.9 and 0.5 litre), adding only another 7 oz. to my load.

Meals need to be kept simple, but can be both nourishing and enjoyable, and if dried food (my breakfast favourite of porridge, raisins and banana slices, for example) is soaked beforehand, little time or fuel is required for cooking

3. Photography

Requiring photographs of a quality suitable for publication or audio-visual presentation has, in the past, meant carrying two SLR camera bodies and at least three interchangeable lenses: a wide-angle of 20 or 24mm., a standard 28-80mm. zoom, and a telephoto zoom of 70-210mm. The Nikon system which I use, however, whilst being extremely good and reliable, is also quite heavy. For this journey I therefore took just one body, an F70, which at 23 oz. is one of the lightest SLR cameras Nikon manufacture, together with a Nikkor 24-120mm. zoom lens. This lens, which is a recent addition to their range, is not only incredibly sharp and quite compact, but, with such a wide zoom range and excellent close-up performance, it is now the only one I need carry, thus making frequent lens changes unnecessary.

Compact cameras are ideal for print film, of course, but seldom match the lens quality and exposure accuracy of SLR cameras demanded by slide film. Two exceptions, both of which I have used regularly, are the tiny Minox GT-E with its brilliantly crisp 35mm. f2.8 lens, and the equally small but more sophisticated Ricoh GR1 which boasts a 28mm. f2.8 lens so suitable for landscapes and equal in optical performance. I took the Ricoh on this walk to use with print film, but could also rest secure in the knowledge that in the unlikely event of the F70 failing, I still had a camera I could use with slide film. Both cameras were carried in a single padded and waterproof 'Lifeventure' camera bag supported by a diagonal neoprene shoulder strap across the chest, giving me instant access to either camera whenever they were required.

Slide film used was Fuji Sensia 1-ASA, and for prints Fuji Superia 200ASA.

Another book by Mike Perrin

Upon High Places

Stories from the mountains of Wales

Out of many years experience climbing the mountains of Wales, Mike Perrin brings us a collection of parable-like stories which open our eyes to God in nature and in grace. These stories evoke the grandeur of God and a sense of the mystery of his ways. They also movingly convey the deep trust in God of someone who has had to face great personal tragedy.

Here are stories which will inspire and encourage fellow pilgrims in their own spiritual journey.

96 pp.
ISBN 1 85049 133 X
published by Bryntirion Press

To Bala for a Bible

**The story of Mary Jones and the
beginnings of the Bible Society**

by

Elisabeth Williams

In 1784 a girl was born in a beautiful valley beneath
the great Mountain of Cadair Idris in North Wales.
She was called Mary Jones. The story of her barefoot
walk to Bala, a small town about twenty-five miles
away, to buy a Bible has made Mary Jones a household name to many. The tale has made a deep impression, not only upon people in Wales, but also upon
people all over the world, where her story is now told
in many different languages.

This book draws on the most reliable sources, including the reminiscences of those who knew her well, in
order to create a lively portrait of Mary Jones and her
background. This has been done, not only in words,
but also with the aid of a wealth of illustrations.

Here is a book which will appeal to young and old
alike.

18 pp.
ISBN 1 85049 050 3
Published by Bryntirion Press

Revival Comes
to Wales

The story of the
1859 Revival in Wales
by
Eifion Evans

This fascinating book traces the background,
development and fruit of this amazing revival, in
which an estimated 110,000 people were converted. Throughout, the author is not concerned with
history alone, but seeks to create in the reader
a longing for similar manifestations of
God's power today.

132 pp.
ISBN 1 85049 025 2
Published by Bryntirion Press

The Welsh Revival
of 1904

by
Eifion Evans

Foreword by D. Martyn Lloyd-Jones

The remarkable story of this powerful revival
and the people associated with it.
Now in its eighth printing.

'A gem, full of excitement, sound judgement and good
instruction.' (*Evangelical Times*)

114 pp.
ISBN 1 85049 037 6
Published by Bryntirion Press